NAMED
BY GOD

NAMED *by* GOD

Discovering the Power
of God's Names for You

MARY FOXWELL LOEKS

Revell
a division of Baker Publishing Group
Grand Rapids, Michigan

© 2010 by Mary Foxwell Loeks

Published by Revell
a division of Baker Publishing Group
P.O. Box 6287, Grand Rapids, MI 49516-6287
www.revellbooks.com

Printed in the United States of America

Library of Congress Cataloging-in-Publication Data
Loeks, Mary Foxwell.
  Named by God : discovering the power of God's names for you / Mary Foxwell Loeks.
    p.   cm.
  ISBN 978-0-8007-3420-6 (pbk.)
  1. God (Christianity)—Name—Meditations. 2. Jesus Christ—Name—Meditations. I. Title.
BT180.N2L644 2010
242′.5—dc22   2009054332

ISBN 978-0-8007-3420-6

Unless otherwise indicated, Scripture is taken from the HOLY BIBLE, NEW INTER-NATIONAL VERSION®. NIV®. Copyright © 1973, 1978, 1984 by International Bible Society. Used by permission of Zondervan. All rights reserved.

Scripture marked CEV is taken from the Contemporary English Version © 1991, 1992, 1995 by American Bible Society. Used by permission.

Scripture marked KJV is taken from the King James Version of the Bible.

Scripture marked Message is taken from *The Message* by Eugene H. Peterson, copyright © 1993, 1994, 1995, 2000, 2001, 2002. Used by permission of NavPress Publishing Group. All rights reserved.

Scripture marked MLB is taken from The Modern Language Bible: The New Berkeley Version in Modern English copyright © 1945, 1959, 1969 by Hendrickson Publishers, Inc. Used by permission. All rights reserved.

Scripture marked NLT is taken from the *Holy Bible*, New Living Translation, copyright © 1996, 2004. Used by permission of Tyndale House Publishers, Inc., Wheaton, Illinois 60189. All rights reserved.

Scripture marked TNIV is taken from the Holy Bible, Today's New International Version™ Copyright © 2001 by International Bible Society. All rights reserved.

10   11   12   13   14   15   16   7   6   5   4   3   2   1

To
Kristin and Julian,
Emily and Aaron,
Allison and J.D.

You are each named and loved by God.
I love you too—this one's for you.
Mom

CONTENTS

Contents

Contents

Will you come and follow me?

Named and empowered,

you are invited

to worship

the one who calls you by name,

who declares

you

are his.

THE BRIDE OF THE LAMB—
HER NEW NAME

Hallelujah!
For our Lord God Almighty reigns.
Let us rejoice and be glad
and give him glory!
For the wedding of the Lamb has come,
and his *bride* has made herself ready.

Revelation 19:7

One of the seven angels . . . said to me [John], "Come,
I will show you the *bride*, the wife of the Lamb."

Revelation 21:9

As a bridegroom rejoices over his *bride*,
so will your God rejoice over you.

Isaiah 62:5

When your words came, I ate them;
they were my joy and my heart's delight,

for I bear your name,
    O Lord God, Almighty.
            Jeremiah 15:16

Of all the truths in Scripture, none is more amazing than this: Jesus desires an intimate and ongoing relationship with us! Jesus, the Lamb, is the Bridegroom. It is he who invites us to be his bride.

Jesus, our Bridegroom, has offered us his name. Even in this twenty-first century, a bride often accepts the name of her bridegroom, taking it as her own. Some of the names we will consider in the pages that follow are names our Bridegroom has shared with us, names such as *light, shepherds, living stones, merciful*, and *priests*. Others are names that reflect some aspect of our relationship with our Bridegroom, such as *co-workers, heirs of God*, and *followers*.

Names were very important during the centuries when the Scriptures were written. They were often meant to reveal the character of the one named. Scripture gives us many names for the Bridegroom, each one highlighting a facet of who he is. It is his character they reveal. But as we continue in union with the Bridegroom, becoming more like him, these shared names can become ours as well.

What is this union that both the prophet Isaiah and the apostle John declare is a cause for rejoicing, even God's rejoicing? It is really a re-union of God with the people he has made. The gift of the Bridegroom's name indicates his desire to be present with his bride, to have her be a part of himself. "I will never leave you nor forsake you," he promises. Further, it indicates his commitment to protect and provide for his bride. She has no cause for worry, assures Jesus, for his Father, who dresses the field lilies in brilliant colors and provides food for the birds, knows her needs and will make ample provision for her (Matt. 6:25–34). The bride who takes her bridegroom's name receives whatever prestige and power his name represents, for this now becomes the name by which she is known. Access to this new name gives the bride of the Lamb tremendous power; the Bridegroom has promised that the Father will give whatever is asked in his name. "Ask and you will receive," he says, "and your joy will be complete" (John 16:24).

There is something else that comes along with marriage to the Bridegroom: his family! Some brides fail to give this fact much forethought. Some wonderful people are included in our Bridegroom's family, people whose company we delight in, people who encourage us and build us up. And there are others, that, well, there are others.

The best wedding days are joy filled. Some of us have known such days. But they are days, and they do come to an end. Not so for the wedding day of this bride! Her Bridegroom is no longer bound to our limited chronology. A thousand years and a day are the same for him (Ps. 90:4). The honeymoon will continue eternally for the Lamb's bride!

Claim the Name

You have been asked to be the bride of Jesus. Have you said yes? Accepting our Bridegroom's proposal means that when we speak of him to others we can speak with confidence and authority because of our relationship with him.

Accepting our Bridegroom's proposal allows us access to all of his resources!

> *Jesus loves me, this I know*
> *For the Bible tells me so.*
> *Thanks be to God! Amen.*

2

ONE

Holy Father, protect them by the power of your name—
the name you gave me—so that they may be *one* as we
are one. . . . My prayer is not for them alone. I pray also
for those who will believe in me through their message,
that all of them may be *one*, Father, just as you are in
me and I am in you. May they also be in us so that the
world may believe that you have sent me.

John 17:11, 20–21

Aoneness that looks like that of our Triune
God! That is what Jesus pleads for in this
extraordinary prayer, one of the few prayers
of Jesus that has been recorded for us.

We see hints of this oneness as we look at the
church of the twenty-first century. Samuel Stone saw
hints of this oneness as he wrote in 1866:

Elect from every nation, yet one o'er all the
  earth,
Her charter of salvation: one Lord, one faith,
  one birth.
One holy name she blesses, partakes one holy
  food,
And to one hope she presses, with every
  strength endued.

"The Church's One Foundation"

Yet few of us have been part of the church for very long before we have also seen, as the poet continues, a church "by schisms rent asunder, by heresies distressed." Remembering how long ago Jesus prayed this prayer, considering the oneness for which he prayed as good as done, should give hope to those of us who become discouraged at how long it seems to take God to answer the prayers we pray.

Jesus' life was a demonstration of what oneness with the Father looks like (John 17:6). This revelation of Yahweh in the person of Jesus stands in contrast to the refusal of the Jewish people even to pronounce, let alone reveal, the holy name. It is the power of this name, which was personified by Jesus, that protects and keeps those who are one and equips them to share the message (John 17:20–21).

This oneness for which Jesus prayed is a within-the-family thing. It is not oneness with everyone without regard for his or her convictions (John 17:9). Rather, it is oneness with those who believe in him (vv. 20–21).

We have a picture of what a oneness of distinct persons is like when we think of our finest musical ensembles, where multiple pitches and multiple voices or instruments blend into one. Two very important characteristics are present when a musical ensemble sounds as one voice: Its members each pay careful attention to the conductor and the score, and its members listen carefully to one another. No voice stands out, yet each voice must be heard. The pitch must be true.

What would the church of Jesus look like if every member had his or her eyes constantly fixed on Jesus, if they paid careful attention to the "score" (John 17:8)? What if every member listened to the others, adjusted as necessary, then listened and kept listening as the music continued to flow? This was Jesus' prayer, "that they may be one."

Claim the Name

Don't let anything keep you from the oneness for which Jesus longed and prayed. Look today for ways to be reconciled and united with other believers in your life.

> *Let the heights of heaven adore him;*
> *Angel hosts his praises sing,*
> *Powers, dominions bow before him*
> *And extol our God and King.*
> *Let no tongue on earth be silent*
> *Every voice in concert ring,*
> *Evermore and evermore. Amen.*
>
> Marcus Aurelius C. Prudentius,
> "Of the Father's Love Begotten," fifth century

3
SALT

You are the *salt* of the earth.
Matthew 5:13

Most of us think of salt as a flavoring with which to season our food. But less than 5 percent of the salt produced in the world each year is used that way. It has been estimated that there are more than fourteen thousand uses for salt.

Our body's cells must have salt to live and do their work, for nearly 1 percent of our cells and blood consists of salt. When medicines are introduced intravenously to our bodies, they are often mixed with a saline solution. Salt has been used throughout history as a preservative. It has been used as an antiseptic and as a water softener. It has been used to make soap and glass and to make paper whiter. For those of us in the cold northern states, it is used to melt ice from our roads and railroad tracks.

During the time Jesus lived on earth, salt was so scarce and precious it was used as money. Roman soldiers often received part of their pay in salt; our word *salary* comes from the Latin *salarium*, meaning "salt." We sometimes ask if someone "is worth his salt" or refer to people we consider good folks as "salt of the earth," perhaps without remembering the source of that statement. A Hebrew baby was often rubbed with salt to ensure it would be healthy. Many peoples, throughout much of their history, have seen salt as a symbol of honor, hospitality, and friendship. Some have also considered salt a symbol of purity.

Salt does not exist for itself. Its purpose is to penetrate and affect that with which it comes in contact. Much of the salt used by Jesus' contemporaries came from the Dead Sea and could be full of impurities that diminished its flavor. Salt can corrode. Salt can destroy. Too much salt or salt used in the wrong way can be a disaster.

My daughter Kristin keeps salt in her sugar bowl. *She* knows it and always uses it appropriately. But one day Grandma Mary was using her kitchen to create a splendid dessert. The shortcake biscuits were made from an old family recipe—the best! The rich cream had been whipped. The strawberries were juicy and red throughout, picked at their peak of perfection. They were washed, sliced, then gently and generously sugared—or so I thought. At last the time came to assemble and serve. Those strawberry shortcakes were beautiful, a pièce de résistance! Liam, my four-year-old grandson and assistant baker, was the first to take a taste. "Yuck!" he pronounced emphatically, for salt had been used instead of sugar. Those strawberry shortcakes were unsalvageable.

"You are the salt of the earth," Matthew quotes Jesus as saying. Used rightly we can bring out the good flavor of those with whom we come in contact. Used rightly we can preserve the best that is around us. Used rightly we are of great value. We are salt. Who is using us? In whose hand do we find ourselves? There is only one good answer to those questions.

Claim the Name

Think of the hospitality you will extend today—perhaps to a family member—as a means of preserving that relationship and adding flavor to it. Don't force those around you to be needlessly on a low-salt diet!

Today we place ourselves in your hand, Lord Jesus. Use us effectively, to the end that your name is praised. Amen.

4

THOMAS

Now *Thomas* (called Didymus), one of the Twelve, was not with the disciples when Jesus came. When the other disciples told him that they had seen the Lord, he declared, "Unless I see the nail marks in his hands and put my finger where the nails were, and put my hand into his side, I will not believe it."

A week later his disciples were in the house again, and *Thomas* was with them. Though the doors were locked, Jesus came and stood among them and said, "Peace be with you!" Then he said to *Thomas*, "Put your finger here; see my hands. Reach out your hand and put it into my side. Stop doubting and believe."

Thomas said to him, "My Lord and my God!"

John 20:24–28

D oubt. It can happen when what you want to believe more than anything else in the world collides with your reason, experience, and sensory data. Doubt. It's what comes first to mind for many people when they think of Jesus' disciple Thomas. "Doubting Thomas" didn't dare let himself accept secondhand the testimony of the other disciples. He needed to see and touch for himself. But before we are too hard on Thomas, we need to acknowledge that doubting is something all of us do sooner or later. It is a passageway through which many of us travel to reach faith. And it is a shoulder along the faith highway where many of us pull off and wait for a time.

"How much longer, LORD, will you forget about me? Will it be forever? How long will you hide? How long must I be confused and miserable all day? How long will my enemies keep beating me down? Please listen, LORD God, and answer my prayers" (Ps. 13:1–3 CEV). Thomas was neither the first nor the last of the people of God to believe he'd been abandoned by the Lord. These questions, asked by the psalmist David, might just as well have been asked by ourselves or one of our acquaintances today.

Thomas saw the wounds of Jesus. He was invited to touch them. His disbelief melted away. The chagrin he likely felt for what he had said earlier became joy, became worship. Thomas then professed his faith in a testimony as powerful as any in Scripture: "My Lord and my God!"

Church tradition indicates that after Pentecost Thomas preached Christ faithfully in ancient Babylon and Persia. It is thought that in approximately AD 52 he sailed to Malabar on the west coast of India. As a result of his ministry, high caste Brahmins as well as others came to faith in Christ, and churches were established. Fifteen hundred years after Thomas was martyred in

Mylapore (Madras), India, Portuguese sailors arrived. They discovered the Mar Thoma church, planted there by Jesus' faith-full disciple Thomas!

Jesus offers a special blessing to those of us who are twenty-first-century Thomases. "Blessed are those who have not seen and yet have believed" (John 20:29).

There is much we simply can't see. The ways of God are often beyond our knowing. Do you have your list of questions you want to ask God? Many of us do. Our "why" questions may throughout time remain a mystery to us. But our God, big enough to receive our fists if we need to pound them, has shoulders broad enough for our tears when we need to shed them. He does respond to our questions. It is often the response given to Job and to Thomas. Look at me! Shift your focus! See who I am! Know that I am here with you!

Then, seeing, there is no more appropriate response than that of Thomas: "My Lord and my God!"

Claim the Name

We have been given the gift of John's Gospel so that we like Thomas "may believe that Jesus is the Christ, the Son of God, and that by believing [we] may have life in his name" (John 20:31). Spend some time considering the apostle John's testimony.

> Lord Jesus,
>   I do believe; help me overcome my unbelief.
> Amen.

Mark 9:24

DEAR *FORGIVEN* CHILDREN

I write to you, *dear children*,
  because your sins have been *forgiven* on account of
  his [Jesus'] name.

                                                    1 John 2:12

So do you think I'm living in sin too?"

Her story had tumbled out: an abusive husband, her adultery, pregnancy, long nights of crying out to God for mercy, divorce, remarriage, two precious children. And now a mother and others who missed no opportunity to tell her she was living in sin. "So do you think I'm living in sin too?"

The small church group was still. It was a heavy, tense stillness. Someone finally broke it. "I think you're living in forgiveness. We all are."

The apostle John writes to assure his readers that God considers them forgiven. He writes "so that you will not sin. But if anybody does sin, we have one who speaks to the father in our defense—Jesus Christ, the Righteous One. He is the atoning sacrifice for our sins, and not only for ours but also for the sins of the whole world" (1 John 2:1–2).

Forgiveness can be offered only by the one who was wronged or by the one who is able to make right the wrong. Jesus Christ, the righteous, as God, is the one wronged. Jesus Christ, the atoning sacrifice, paid dearly to right our very great wrong. Our debt has been canceled.

The other adjective used by the apostle John in this short but powerful sentence is the word *dear*. We are dear to God! What an amazing truth! The forgiveness offered God's children is not given grudgingly or re-luctantly. There is no hint that God harbors unspoken reservations like we humans sometimes do. "That was a Wedgewood vase you broke, a wedding present from my grandmother." No, God loves us so dearly that the cost to God of our forgiveness is as good as forgotten. But we, the recipients of forgiveness, ought not be so quick to forget its cost.

Forgiveness is a gift, and as with all gifts there is an offer, then either an acceptance or a rejection. An unaccepted gift does not negate the offering. Jesus encourages us to remember the offered forgiveness whenever we pray. "Forgive us our debts," we are told to pray in Matthew 6:12. It isn't as though God withdraws the gift and we have to keep asking for it. It is that we need to be always mindful that we are forgiven children and that as children we still sin and need forgiveness. That mindfulness is what shapes our response to others. "As we also have forgiven our debtors" (Matt. 6:12) is how we are told our prayer is to continue. That we as kingdom citizens accept the holy God's forgiveness is demonstrated as we daily forgive the lesser debts of others. We, all of us, God's dear children, are living in forgiveness!

Claim the Name

Forgiveness is a gift God gives to his children. As with all gifts, the appropriate response is to receive it and to say thank you. Today find a way to thank God for his forgiveness of your sin.

Praise, my soul, the King of heaven;
To his feet your tribute bring.
Ransomed, healed, restored, forgiven,
Evermore his praises sing.
Alleluia, alleluia! Praise the everlasting King!

Fatherlike he tends and spares us;
Well our feeble frame he knows.
In his hand he gently bears us,
Rescues us from all our foes.
Alleluia, alleluia! Widely yet his mercy flows!
*   Amen.*

Henry F. Lyte,
"Praise, My Soul, the King of Heaven," 1834

6

BRANCHES

Jesus said to his disciples: "I am the true vine, and my Father is the gardener. He cuts away every branch of mine that doesn't produce fruit. But he trims clean every branch that does produce fruit, so that it will produce even more fruit. You are already clean because of what I have said to you. Stay joined to me, and I will stay joined to you. Just as a branch cannot produce fruit unless it stays joined to the vine, you cannot produce fruit unless you stay joined to me. I am the vine, and you are the *branches*. If you stay joined to me, and I stay joined to you, then you will produce lots of fruit. But you cannot do anything without me."

John 15:1–5 CEV

Incarnation
Sin severed branches;
fruitless, useless, lifeless, we
by THE BRANCH are healed.

This poem in the form of a Japanese haiku came to me during the night of a wild windstorm as I listened to branches crack and fall from the trees outside. Fierce winds from the spring storm severed a branch, but instead of falling to the ground, it got caught among the other branches. All summer long it kept its green leaves, looking healthy and whole to all but the most observant. Appearances aside, however, that branch was as good as dead, because it had no means of accessing water and nourishment.

The vine (or trunk, or stem) is the life-bringing conduit connecting the branches with the nutrients and moisture of the soil. Fruitfulness is impossible unless a branch remains connected to the vine. Jesus said, "I am the vine; you are the branches" (John 15:5). But near the beginning of time, sin's fierce winds snapped off all human branches from that which was their life. The branches were as good as dead. Then a miracle, unprecedented and unmatched since, took place. Jesus, himself the vine, became "the man whose name is the Branch" (Zech. 6:12) in order that the severed branches might be regrafted into the life-giving vine. "I am the true vine," Jesus tells his disciples, "and my Father is the gardener" (John 15:1).

And our Father is truly a Master Gardener—one who expertly prunes, weeds, waters, and fertilizes the once lifeless branches! He takes the garbage of our lives—the training we think was wasted, the mistakes we've made, the experiences we regret—and makes of it the finest compost. This he works carefully into the soil, which nourishes us. In and with all things this Master Gardener works, tirelessly and patiently. We branches tend to lose heart. We become impatient. Being pruned hurts. We don't think nearly as much needs to be cut. If *we* were the gardener, we'd never do it this way! But we remain joined to the vine, because the vine remains joined to us. And sometimes, to our amazement, we branches begin to bear fruit—fruit that will last!

Claim the Name

Have you observed (human) branches who think they know better than the Master Gardener? What was the result? Read and reflect on John 15:1–17 as you determine what abiding in the vine will look like for you today.

> *Master Gardener God,*
> *May we, being rooted and established in love, have power, together with all the saints, to grasp how wide and long and high and deep is the love of Christ, and to know this love that surpasses knowledge—that we may be filled to the measure of all the fullness of God. Amen.*
>
> Ephesians 3:17–19, adapted

7

FREE

So if the Son sets you *free*, you will be *free* indeed.

John 8:36 TNIV

You, my brothers and sisters, were called to be *free*. But do not use your freedom to indulge the sinful nature; rather serve one another humbly in love. For the entire law is fulfilled in keeping this one command: "Love your neighbor as yourself."

Galatians 5:13–14 TNIV

The little old woman crouched near the row of tightly woven covered baskets. Spotting the young American visitors to Thailand, she called out to them: "Escuse me, ma'ams. Set birds free? One hundred baht—bring you good luck!" One of the high school students, charmed by the notion of setting a basket of baby birds free, paid the requested one hundred baht. She received one of the baskets and lifted the lid, releasing the little captives it contained.

Paying for freedom is not as unusual as it might at first seem, for freedom is rarely free. Someone has had to pay for it. Jesus, the Son, has released us from the captivity of sin. It cost him dearly to purchase our freedom.

Freedom doesn't mean "without limits." Often the limits are the very things that free us, as the namers of a Grand Rapids, Michigan, business called Freedom Fencing were mindful. A fenced-in yard frees a young child to play outdoors safely, despite the traffic rushing by on the street. The glass walls of an aquarium contain the water that is vital to the life of the fish swimming freely within them. Practicing a musical instrument for four to six hours daily severely limits a musician's other activities. But it is that practice that frees him or her to make glorious music.

There is a sense in which God's commandments are "freedom fences." To have no other gods is a fence, yet it frees us to pour all our worship, all our praise, undiluted and undistracted, at the feet of our one Triune God. Not lying is a fence, yet it frees us to be truth speakers and to pursue a relationship with the one who is Truth. Not breaking our marriage vows is a fence, yet it frees us to give ourselves exclusively to our marriage partner. Not coveting is a fence, yet it frees us to focus on that for which we can give thanks. We may not understand or appreciate the freedom fences. We are too much like the little girl who pushed and banged against the gate that kept her from falling down a steep flight of steps.

The apostle Paul tells us why we have been freed. It is to serve one another humbly in love. The entire law, writes Paul, is fulfilled in keeping this one command: "Love your neighbor as yourself," a love only possible as it flows from being loved by and loving God. Any other exercise of our freedom will destroy us. Any other exercise of our freedom would be like freeing a tropical fish from its aquarium to have full run of the house.

Thank God for the freedom purchased for you at such great cost. Stop beating against the fences!

> Lord Jesus,
> I run in the path of your commands,
>   for you have set my heart free.
> Teach me, O LORD, to follow your decrees;
>   then I will keep them to the end. Amen.
>
> Psalm 119:32–33

8

SIMON PETER

Jesus . . . looked at him and said, "You are *Simon* son of
John. You will be called *Cephas*" (which, when trans-
lated, is *Peter*).

John 1:42
(Cephas [Aramaic] = Petros [Greek] = Rock [English])

Simon Peter answered, "You are the Christ, the Son of
the living God."

Jesus replied, "Blessed are you, *Simon* son of Jonah,
for this was not revealed to you by man, but by my
Father in heaven. And I tell you that you are Peter, and
on this rock I will build my church, and the gates of
Hades will not overcome it. I will give you the keys of
the kingdom of heaven."

Matthew 16:16–19

Exhausted after hours of battling yet another of Galilee's sudden evening storms, the disciples distrusted their own eyes. What was this apparition moving toward them, apparently walking on water? The figure moved closer and closer! They shrieked in fear, "It has to be a ghost!" Their shuddering and shivering were due at least as much to terror as to the wet and cold of the early morning air.

Then over the howling wind and surging sea they heard a familiar voice. "Take courage! It is I. Don't be afraid."

Impulsive and impetuous, Simon, nicknamed Peter, shouted back, "Lord, if it's really you, tell me to come to you on the water."

"Come," Jesus invited.

Defying common sense, the laws of gravity and buoyancy, even his own nickname (Rock), Peter, disciple of Jesus, stepped out of the boat and began to walk toward Jesus on top of the water!

But then he saw the wind. He saw the waves. It occurred to him how crazy and impossible a thing this was. As he began to be afraid he began to sink. "Lord, save me!" he yelled. Immediately Jesus reached out his hand, caught Peter, pulled him to safety, and chided him for doubting.

Once they were inside the boat the wind died down. Peter, wet and shivering, joined the others as they offered Jesus their worship, exclaiming, "Truly you are the Son of God!"

Simon, son of John (Jonas), had been given one of the most commonly used names in first-century Palestine, so to distinguish him from all the other Simons, he had somehow acquired the Greek nickname

Petros, or Rock. Petros (Peter) was virtually unknown as a personal name at the time—a unique name for a truly unique individual!

Peter is mentioned in the New Testament more often than any of the other disciples, and two of his letters are included in the scriptural canon. Matthew is the only one of the Gospel writers who includes this short snapshot of Peter walking on the water toward Jesus, but it offers us insight into the person Simon Peter was when he first came to know Jesus. Peter was no rock when Jesus first met him. He wavered between confidence and cowardice. His bursts of faith-filled insight were punctuated and punctured by doubt and denials.

But Jesus knew what God himself would do as Peter learned to keep his eyes on Jesus. Jesus seized the nickname Petros and transformed it into a benediction!

"You are blessed, Simon, with insight from the father God. You will indeed be a rock, steady and firm. I will begin building my church with you, Peter-rock," announced Jesus. "You are its *steward*. You hold the keys that access all of heaven's resources. Even all of death's power will be no match for those resources!"

Peter, the Rock, knew who the Chief Rock was (1 Peter 2:4–7). It was to this Rock that he pointed those to whom he spoke and wrote until he himself was crucified.

Claim the Name

As we too keep our eyes on Jesus, we will begin to be rocks, stable and solid, not washed away by a storm.

As rocks we will be able to share with others a safe and sure place to stand.

> *[May we] grow in the grace and knowledge of our Lord and Savior Jesus Christ. To him be glory both now and forever! Amen.*
>
> 2 Peter 3:18

STEWARDS

Moreover it is required in *stewards*, that a man [or woman] be found faithful.

1 Corinthians 4:2 KJV

Use hospitality one to another without grudging. As every man [or woman] hath received the gift, even so minister the same one to another, as good *stewards* of the manifold grace of God.

1 Peter 4:9–10 KJV

Stewards. It's not a name we encounter often in our twenty-first-century egalitarian culture— except on board ship. For missionary families with limited budgets heading for Japan in the late 1940s through the 1960s, travel by ship was often the best option. So we in the Foxwell family learned about stewards at a very young age.

Dining-room stewards served us delicious meals—and we didn't have to do the dishes! Stewards offered little cups of sherbet at 10:00 a.m., and stewards on British ships served high tea punctually at 4:00 p.m. Our steward even made our beds in the morning. Stewards would bring us an extra blanket or towel if we needed one, and the stewards' keys unlocked the cabinets in which the ship's books and games were kept.

"Do the stewards own the ship?" I asked one day.

"No," was the reply. "Their job is to take care of all the things and people on board the ship."

Stewards. We don't own the ship, but we have keys to access everything on board. That access is meant to equip us for serving. God expects us to be faithful caretakers of both our world and the material things entrusted to us.

The apostle Peter reminds us stewards of the relationship between good stewardship and hospitality. How can I help? What does that person need? What do I have that I could use to meet that need? What necessary job is being overlooked? These are the kinds of questions good stewards ought always to be asking.

And we have been made stewards of God's many-faceted grace. We need to understand that everything else over which we have been made stewards—not owners—is meant to be an expression of God's grace. We are not to hoard this grace for our own exclusive use. We are not to keep it locked away in a closet, inaccessible to anyone. We are to dispense God's grace generously, just as good stewards on ships dispense blankets, sherbet, and games.

Being a steward is a blend of servant and manager. As managers we are God's appointed agents; we have the authority to act on God's behalf. As servants—the best managers always are good servants—we focus on the other person's needs. We are the conduit between the owner and those we are to serve. How well we do our job reflects on the one to whom we belong. We have been entrusted with all of God's resources. We are recipients of God's grace. We also hold God's grace in our hands so that we may share it with others. It is a requirement that we be found faithful!

Claim the Name

To claim this name is to remember three things: First, we are not the owners. Second, the owner wants that over which we are stewards to be used faithfully (Matt. 25:18, 24–26). Third, being a steward points those we serve to the grace of their host—the living God.

> Gracious God,
>   Make us faithful stewards of your grace this day. Amen.

10
GOD'S MASTERPIECE

For we are *God's masterpiece*. He has created us anew in Christ Jesus, so we can do the good things he planned for us long ago.

Ephesians 2:10 NLT

Then the Lord God formed the man from the dust of the ground. He breathed the breath of life into the man's nostrils, and the man became a living person.

Genesis 2:7 NLT

Therefore, if anyone is in Christ, . . . [that one] is a new creation; the old has gone, the new has come!

2 Corinthians 5:17

When I look at the night sky and see the work of your
      fingers—
  the moon and the stars you set in place—

> what are mere mortals that you should think about
>   them,
> human beings that you should care for them?
>
> Psalm 8:3–4 NLT

The psalmist opens up for us God's art portfolio (Psalm 8). Take a look, he invites. The heavens. The moon and the stars. All flocks and herds. All the birds of the air and the fish of the sea—each is a brilliant example of God's creativity, each a work of God's fingers. But God's masterpiece? That into which God poured his own spirit? That which gives the best hint of what God is like (Gen. 1:26–27)? God's masterpiece can be seen if we look in a mirror. God's masterpiece can be seen in the person sitting next to us. Nothing has been spared in our making. Truly we are fearfully and wonderfully made (Ps. 139:14)!

The apostle Paul reminds us that as God's masterpiece we were not created to hang on a wall, bordered by a handsome frame, or to perch proudly on a pedestal. What does it mean for us that we are "created . . . anew in Christ Jesus, so we can do the good things he planned for us long ago" (Eph. 2:10 NLT)? One word summarizes it: *praise*. Praise means more than the singing that takes place before the sermon on a Sunday morning. All the rest of God's portfolio praises him without any prodding. "The heavens declare the glory of God; the skies proclaim the work of his hands" (Ps. 19:1). We are the only part of creation that may choose. But the truth remains that it was God's intent from before time that our serving, our creating, our employment, our thought life, our use of the internet—all be used to praise our Creator.

43

Even though many of us don't consider ourselves artists and if asked, "What have you created?" would respond negatively, our ability to create is a quality God put into his masterpiece creation, ourselves. Think for a moment: What have you put something of yourself into? A garden? A handmade card? A lovingly rebuilt classic car? A quilt? A book? A bookshelf? A special meal? A poem? All of these represent someone's workmanship. An understandable bond forms between the creator and the creation.

Now imagine this: What if your masterpiece—that into which you have poured your time and creative energy—is ruined? Your painting is rained on. Your Corvette is totaled. Bold graphite pencil marks the quilt into which you have put hundreds of hours. Your dog gets to that special dinner before you do. And—if you are God—your people are ruined by sin. Some creators would give up at this point.

Potters, however, have a way of taking a ruined creation, even after it has dried or been fired, and reprocessing it so something new can be made from that clay.

The Creator God did not give up on his ruined masterpiece. Jesus Christ came to restore and renew it! So if anyone is in Christ, that person "is a new creation; the old has gone, the new has come!" (2 Cor. 5:17). In Jesus Christ we are twice God's masterpiece!

Claim the Name

Trust. Rest. Wonder! Being God's masterpiece is not about you. It has everything to do with who God is and what God is doing. Praise God today.

Master Artist God,

We praise you because we have been fearfully and wonderfully made and remade. Your works are wonderful, we know that full well. May our works bring you praise this day. Amen.

THE REDEEMED OF THE LORD

Give thanks to the LORD, for he is good;
    his love endures forever.
Let *the redeemed of the LORD* say this—
    those he redeemed from the hand of the foe.

                                    Psalm 107:1–2

They will be called "The Holy People"
    and "*The People Redeemed by the LORD.*"
And Jerusalem will be known as "The Desirable Place"
    and "The City No Longer Forsaken."

                                    Isaiah 62:12 NLT

Redeemed. Redemption. Do those sometimes feel like "church words," just a bit removed from our daily lives?

Then visit with me a pawnshop in West Michigan. Its shelves and glass cases contain just about anything:

chain saws, fine jewelry, musical instruments, lawn mowers, toys, electronic equipment. As the proprietor said, "Anything I can sell for a profit." About half the time, someone returns to this shop to redeem the item he or she has pawned. Always it will be more expensive than the value originally placed on the item. Redemption is very costly.

If someone simply wanted a little extra cash, it would be far preferable to part with unneeded items at a garage sale, or to use an online sales service, or to place an ad in a local newspaper. No one redeems something unless he or she truly wants it back!

"To redeem" is to buy back, to reclaim, to rescue. Our Redeemer, Jesus, has done all this for us. Our redemption came at horrific cost—it cost Jesus his life and momentary separation from the Father. For reasons we will likely never fully comprehend, our redemption was undertaken at the initiative and according to the will of the Triune God. No one redeems something without truly wanting it back!

We the redeemed dare not keep quiet about it, for we the redeemed have every reason to give thanks.

Twice Sealed

Examine God's portfolio:
Stars and sunsets, moon, rainbows,
Humming birds and buffalo,
Whales in oceans far below.
Then at last, the masterpiece!
Creation's work with us did cease.
Just humankind received God's seal—
God's image in us is revealed.
Sin entered God's portfolio
And dealt God's art a dreadful blow.

47

Our Maker we could never know,
Into his presence never go.
But God, his masterpiece once lost,
Redeemed it at tremendous cost.
We're Spirit-sealed—proof we're reclaimed,
And thus twice sealed with God's own name.

MARY FOXWELL LOEKS, BASED ON EPHESIANS 2:10;
GENESIS 1:26–27; 2:2; EPHESIANS 1:13–14

Japanese artists "sign" their work by stamping it with a seal, or han. At one time it was the custom for the first purchaser of the work also to seal it with a han.

Claim the Name

The psalmist has told us how to claim this name! "Give thanks unto the Lord, for he is good; . . . Let the redeemed of the Lord say this" (Ps. 107:1–2)

Jesus, my Redeemer, name above all names,
Precious Lamb of God, Messiah, hope for sinners slain.
Thank you, O my Father, for giving us your Son,
And leaving your Spirit till the work on earth is done. Amen.

12

MARTHA

As Jesus and his disciples were on their way, he came to a village where a woman named *Martha* opened her home to him. . . .

But *Martha* was distracted by all the preparations that had to be made. She came to him [Jesus] and asked, "Lord, don't you care that my sister has left me to do the work by myself? Tell her to help me!"

"*Martha, Martha,*" the Lord answered, "you are worried and upset about many things, but only one thing is needed. Mary has chosen what is better, and it will not be taken away from her."

Luke 10:38, 40–42

Thirteen extra guests for dinner and probably for the night too! First-century Bethany did not offer pizza delivery or Chinese takeout. Martha, whose strength is taking charge and getting things done, kicks into high gear. Extra bread will need to be baked—those disciples are always hungry! Someone will have to talk the wine merchant up the street into selling them several more jars. Another lamb will need to be butchered and cooked. And the stew needs something else—are there any more leeks in the garden? And yes, someone must be sent to carry more water from the well. Washing the feet of her guests will not be overlooked at Martha's house. It's for Jesus after all, and Martha wants everything to be done right.

If Jesus had a favorite place to hang out, it was probably Martha's house. There he could shed his sandals and be at home. There he could relax and unwind. Martha, Mary, and Lazarus loved him and were his dear friends. He could trust them with his weariness. He could trust them with what burdened his heart. That Jesus found this home so welcoming was in large measure due to Martha's hard work. Martha used well her gift of hospitality (John 12:2).

Hospitality is a spiritual gift. Elders are urged to use this gift (1 Tim. 3:2; Titus 1:8), as are all believers (1 Peter 4:9). Sometimes the words *hospitality* and *entertainment* are used interchangeably. The two include many of the same ingredients—food, drink, perhaps music, edifying words, a gathering place. And there is physical work, including food preparation. Organizational details are also involved in both. But there is an important difference. Hospitality is always about the one being served. Entertainment is more of a performance, with the spotlight on the one doing the entertaining. The hospitable Martha has for the moment lost her focus. Her own needs and frustrations have taken center stage instead of the needs of her guests. This is why Jesus admonishes her. "I can do without anything that leaves you harried and hassled," Jesus wants to assure Martha. "Time with you is what I most prize."

Jesus is not unmindful of the tasks that need to be done. The "Martha-tasks" when offered without grumbling (1 Peter 4:9) can be love-gifts to the people being served as well as love-gifts offered to Jesus. But Martha, and we twenty-first-century Marthas, need to remember where true hospitality must focus.

Claim the Name

Martha, keep it simple.

Use your organizational skills to accomplish all you can ahead of time.

DO-ing and PRAY-ing are not mutually exclusive; making soup can be a form of prayer.

Serving peanut butter sandwiches and handing guests the sheets to make their own beds is okay.

It is time with you that your guests will most prize.

Serving your sister graciously could be both a love-gift for her as well as a form of serving Jesus!

Martha, it's not about you.

Lord Jesus,
Take my life and let it be consecrated, Lord, to
thee.

*Take my moments and my days; let them flow in
   endless praise.*
*Take my hands and let them move at the impulse
   of thy love.*
*Take my feet and let them be swift and beautiful
   for thee. Amen.*

Frances Ridley Havergal, "Take My Life and Let It Be," 1874

13

MARY OF BETHANY

As Jesus and his disciples were on their way, he came to a village where a woman named Martha opened her home to him. She had a sister called *Mary*, who sat at the Lord's feet listening to what he said.

Luke 10:38–39

A dinner was given in Jesus' honor. Martha served, while Lazarus was among those reclining at the table with him. Then *Mary* took about a pint of pure nard, an expensive perfume; she poured it on Jesus' feet and wiped his feet with her hair. And the house was filled with the fragrance of the perfume.

But one of his disciples, Judas Iscariot, who was later to betray him, objected, "Why wasn't this perfume sold and the money given to the poor? It was worth a year's wages." . . .

"Leave her alone," Jesus replied. "It was meant that she should save this perfume for the day of my burial.

You will always have the poor among you, but you will
not always have me."

John 12:2–5, 7–8

As they have done many times before, Jesus
and his disciples stop in Bethany to savor
the hospitality and refreshment they know
they will receive at the home of Lazarus, Martha, and
Mary. No one else knows, but the Passover Feast they
will soon observe will be the last one Jesus spends
with his disciples. Once again a lovely meal is prepared, and Martha serves. If anyone other than Jesus
hears the rumbling thunder of the storm that awaits
Jesus in Jerusalem, nothing is said of it.

No words spoken by Mary are recorded for us in
Scripture, unlike her more extroverted elder sister.
Listening seems to be Mary's love offering. Because
she listens with an open, loving heart, she hears
and understands what the disciples, though they
have heard all the same words, have missed. Mary
somehow knows that Jesus' death is imminent. She
senses the moments of anguish that punctuate his
calm, determined purpose. Jesus will submit to the
unthinkable because there is no alternative. Martha
has verbally testified that she believes Jesus is the
resurrection (John 11:25, 27). Mary's extravagant
gesture indicates that she understands that for there
to be a resurrection there must first be a death.

Mary models for us what it means to worship
truly. She understands that prayer—communing
with God—*is* doing something. Praying is work.
Mary brings to her worship an open, loving heart.

She listens and hears. She recognizes and acknowledges who the Lord is. And Mary responds. She gives what she has, and in doing so she gives herself. Her act of worship is costly—a whole year's wages! Perhaps it might otherwise have been her dowry. She breaks the flask of costly ointment and pours it—all of it—on Jesus' feet. As acts of worship often seem to those who merely watch, not worshiping, her act appears foolish. What a terrible waste! Think of what she *could* have done with it! As the fragrant aroma fills the room, Mary loosens her long hair—"Scandalous!" mutter the nonworshipers—and with it she begins, wordlessly, to caress the feet of Jesus.

A few of the guests move to stop Mary, to bring an end to this scene, which both embarrasses them and provokes their indignation, but Jesus overrules. "Let her be," he insists. "She is doing what she can to prepare my body for burial."

"Burial?" the others could have exclaimed. "What are you talking about? You aren't going to be buried any time soon!" Though they had heard Jesus' teachings, once again they had not heard the words beneath his words.

Only one thing is needed. Mary has chosen what is better, and it will not be taken away from her.

Claim the Name

Would-be Marys

How often is open-hearted listening part of your worship?

> Does your worship ever involve offering something that comes at great cost to you?
>
> Do you ever forget that praying *is* doing something?

Mary-types

Even in the twenty-first-century church, Marthas have a hard time understanding Marys, and to some extent vice versa. It is important for those who claim this name to reach out to the Marthas. If you were to carry tomorrow's water home from the well, it could be a love-gift for your sister. It might even make Jesus smile.

> *Lord Jesus,*
> *Take my heart—it is thine own; it shall be thy royal throne.*
> *Take my love; my Lord, I pour at thy feet its treasure store.*
> *Take myself, and I will be ever, only, all for thee.*
> *Ever, only, all for thee. Amen.*
>
> Frances Ridley Havergal, "Take My Life and Let It Be," 1874

14

CLAY

Yet, O LORD, you are our Father.
   We are the *clay*, you are the potter;
   we are all the work of your hand.

Isaiah 64:8

Who are you, a mere human being, to argue with God?
Should the thing that was created say to the one who
created it, "Why have you made me like this?" When a
potter makes jars out of *clay*, doesn't he have a right to
use the same lump of *clay* to make one jar for decora-
tion and another to throw garbage into?

Romans 9:20–21 NLT

But we have this treasure [the light of God's glory] in
jars of *clay* to show that this all-surpassing power is
from God and not from us.

2 Corinthians 4:7

Ouch! I don't like the way you're pressing and squeezing me! . . .

That's to work the air bubbles out, you say? So I won't crack later on? Oh . . .

You wouldn't *throw* me on that moving wheel, would you? It's spinning so fast; I'm not ready for anything like that yet . . .

But you're ready. And that's all that matters? Hmmm . . . Hey! This hurts! Don't you think about my feelings at all? . . .

Check out the scars in the Potter's hands . . . What kind of an answer is that anyway? . . .

I don't think I like being this shape. And while we're on that subject, the color of the glaze you've chosen for me isn't at all becoming, if you ask me . . .

You didn't ask me? Oh . . .

Surely you aren't going to make me just another ordinary water pot, are you? I had so hoped to be something unique—a priceless *objet d'art* . . .

Wait a minute! You weren't planning to put me in the kiln, were you? It's hot in there! Why, if I do get out of that oven, I won't ever be the same again! . . .

That was your plan, you say? To make me strong and usable? A jar to hold living water? To show that this all-surpassing power is from God and not from . . . Oh, I think I'm beginning to see.

Claim the Name

Good clay is soft, moist, and shapeable. Is *shapeable* a word that might be used to describe you? Do you know who is shaping you?

Have you been broken, or perhaps you've dried out? There is a process by which potters can take broken pots, or dried-out clay, and make them usable once again!

Even cracked pots can let the light of God's glory shine through!

> *Have thine own way, Lord! . . .*
> *Thou art the potter, I am the clay.*
> *Mold me and make me after thy will,*
> *While I am waiting, yielded and still.*
>
> *Have thine own way, Lord! . . .*
> *Hold o'er my being absolute sway.*
> *Fill with thy Spirit till all shall see*
> *Christ only, always, living in me. Amen.*

Adelaide A. Pollard,
"Have Thine Own Way, Lord," 1907

A DOORKEEPER

Better is one day in your courts
    than a thousand elsewhere;
I would rather be a *doorkeeper* in the house of my
        God
    than dwell in the tents of the wicked.

Psalm 84:10

The psalmist is expressing his deep yearning to be in God's presence—to be near God, even if for only a day.

He may have been a Levite who had served in the temple prior to his being taken captive. In any case, he is now far from the physical place that had represented the presence of God to him. He prays a blessing on the pilgrims journeying to Jerusalem, longing to be with them. He even envies the birds who have unlimited access to and can build nests in the holy places where Israel was to have communion with God.

The psalmist, humble though his work in the temple may have been, nonetheless longs for the sweet nearness to God he experienced in the past.

Consider doorkeepers you may have observed. They probably weren't the CEOs of their companies, or the owners of their hotels, or the senior pastors of their churches. But a doorkeeper is often the first to offer a greeting or a welcome. A doorkeeper may offer to help you with the load you are carrying or to shelter you with an umbrella. A good doorkeeper is able to answer questions and to offer information and directions. A doorkeeper spots potential trouble and summons help. Doorkeepers are often easy to identify because of their attire; their uniforms tell us whom they serve, and their very presence indicates, should there be any question, where the door is, for a doorkeeper is near the door.

What about us? What kind of doorkeeper would we be? Are we welcoming, even to strangers (Matt. 25:35)? Do we seek those whose burdens are heavy and offer to carry those burdens (Gal. 6:2)? Can we give a reason for the hope that is within us (1 Peter 3:15)? Do we know where to go for help (Ps. 121:1–2)? Are we identified with the one whose name we bear because we are clothed in his garments of compassion, kindness, humility, gentleness, and patience (Col. 3:12)? Do we yearn to be near the Door (John 10:9 KJV)? What kind of doorkeeper would we be?

Perhaps doorkeeper is not a name we want to claim. Perhaps our thought life, our use of time, our use of money, or our desires make us a little squeamish about being too near God, too near God's scrutiny. We are uncomfortable with the notion of being in God's presence. Or perhaps we long for a name a bit more prestigious, work we perceive as more significant than that of a humble doorkeeper. We don't really want to be near the Door.

All of us who belong to God—whether CEOs or doorkeepers, whether entrusted with one or two or five talents—are servants. The name doorkeeper is the psalmist's way of describing his own work. But it is not our work itself that concerns God; it is our faithfulness in doing it. At the end of the day, that faithfulness is what brings God pleasure and will elicit his commendation, "Well done, good and faithful servant! You have been faithful with a few things; I will put you in charge of many things. Come and share your master's happiness!" (Matt. 25:21). In the end the psalmist will receive that for which his heart longs. So will we.

Claim the Name

In what specific ways can a twenty-first-century person such as yourself be near the Door (John 10:9 KJV)? Write down two specific ways in which you will seek to be near the Door today.

> *Hear my prayer, O LORD God Almighty;*
> *listen to me, O God of Jacob. . . .*
> *Better is one day in your courts*
> *than a thousand elsewhere;*
> *I would rather be a doorkeeper in the house of*
> *my God*
> *than dwell in the tents of the wicked. Amen.*
>
> Psalm 84:8, 10

16

HOLY

I am the LORD your God; consecrate yourselves and be *holy*, because I am *holy*. . . . I am the LORD who brought you up out of Egypt to be your God; therefore be *holy*, because I am *holy*.

Leviticus 11:44–45

To the church of God in Corinth, to those sanctified in Christ Jesus and called to be *holy*, together with all those everywhere who call on the name of our Lord Jesus Christ—their Lord and ours.

1 Corinthians 1:2

But just as he who called you is *holy*, so be *holy* in all you do; for it is written: "Be *holy*, because I am *holy*."

1 Peter 1:15–16

How many conversations about being holy take place today in office break rooms, over backyard fences, or around kitchen tables? If there were an internet site tagged "Being Holy," how many hits do you suppose it would generate? Have we, called by God to be a holy people, made holiness into an anachronism?

Those few flaws and blemishes we have help us fit in better with everybody else, don't they? And being a little tarnished seems so much more fashionable! We surely wouldn't want anyone to think we consider ourselves "holier than thou."

People of God, we dare not delude ourselves! Holiness is not optional. Holiness is not possible to achieve on our own. And holiness is not primarily about us.

One of the primary themes of the book of Leviticus is holiness. Much of this Old Testament book contains detailed directions concerning the rituals and procedures God's people were to follow in order to be holy. And the command is clear: "Therefore be holy, because I am holy." There is no "how would you like to . . ." or "don't you think maybe . . ." about it. And lest we think being holy was something only for people of Old Testament time, the apostles Paul and Peter pick up the theme, quoting Leviticus. Being holy is the only way we can have a relationship with God. It is not optional.

But we cannot achieve holiness on our own. The prophet Isaiah had a vision of the holy God, which he describes in Isaiah 6. As the seraphim called to one another, "Holy, holy, holy is the LORD Almighty; the whole earth is full of his glory," the doorposts and thresholds shook and the temple was filled with smoke. Isaiah cried out in terror, "Woe to me! . . . I am ruined! For I am a man of unclean lips, and I live among a people of unclean lips, and my eyes have seen the King, the LORD Almighty" (vv. 3, 5). Becoming holy was not something Isaiah could achieve on his own. Nor could the apostle Paul, who reminds us that "all have sinned and fall short of the glory of God" (Rom. 3:23). No amount of struggling and striving on our part can result in our holiness.

Yet God calls us to be holy. Holy is one of our Bridegroom's names. Our relationship with him depends on our claiming this name. Yet when we catch even a glimpse of God's holiness, we have every reason to respond as Isaiah did. How is it possible then for us to be holy?

One day when Moses was out caring for his father-in-law's sheep, he saw a bush that continued to be green even though it was ablaze with fire. A voice warned him: "Do not come any closer. . . . Take off your sandals, for the place where you are standing is holy ground" (Exod. 3:5). There was nothing unique about that particular patch of ground. It was not intrinsically holy. That ground was made holy by the presence of God. Likewise, it is not some intrinsic quality we have but rather the presence of God with us and in us that makes us holy!

The church in Corinth was made up of many flawed individuals. There were some serious problems in that congregation. But these Corinthians were called to be holy because Jesus Christ is holy. Holy people haven't always been particularly good people, as this church illustrates. The prophet Isaiah was a flawed individual who received the touch of God in the form of a live coal. That touch represented atonement for his sin and made him holy and thus usable by God.

For Isaiah, Paul, the church at Corinth, and for us, holiness is a gift offered by God to be received. It is the touch of God on our lips that makes us holy. It is the presence of God in our lives that keeps us holy.

Claim the Name

Members of the Sanhedrin "took note that . . . [Peter and Paul] had been with Jesus" (Acts 4:13). That is the result of holiness—those around us note that we have been with Jesus.

Choose an area of your life where you would like Jesus' presence to be more evident. Spend time in prayer, asking God to show you what actions to take to make this a reality.

> *Breathe on me, breath of God, fill me with life anew,*
> *That I may love the way you love, and do what you would do.*
>
> *Breathe on me, breath of God, until my heart is pure,*
> *Until my will is one with yours, to do and to endure.*
>
> *Breathe on me, breath of God, so shall I never die,*
> *But live with you the perfect life for all eternity. Amen.*
>
> Edwin Hatch, "Breathe on Me, Breath of God," 1878

BARTIMAEUS

As Jesus and his disciples, together with a large crowd, were leaving . . . [Jericho], a blind man, *Bartimaeus* (that is, the son of Timaeus), was sitting by the roadside begging. When he heard that it was Jesus of Nazareth, he began to shout, "Jesus, Son of David, have mercy on me!" . . .

Jesus stopped and said, "Call him."

So they called to the blind man, "Cheer up! On your feet! He's calling you." Throwing his cloak aside, he jumped to his feet and came to Jesus.

"What do you want me to do for you?" Jesus asked him.

The blind man said, "Rabbi, I want to see."

"Go," said Jesus, "your faith has healed you." Immediately he received his sight and followed Jesus along the road.

Mark 10:46–47, 49–52

J esus, Son of David, have mercy on me!" The repeatedly shouted words had their desired effect. Jesus stopped to listen. So few understood who he was and why he was here. Even the disciples he'd mentored over the last three years didn't seem to get it. Jesus was on his way to Jerusalem to observe Passover with those disciples. He alone knew that what awaited him there would be much more than feast and celebration. This would be the week the Son of David would accomplish the mission for which he had come. This would be the week that would make the outpouring of God's mercy possible.

"Jesus, Son of David, have mercy!" The very presence of a blind beggar was a nuisance; his shouting was obnoxious. But all attempts to rebuke and silence him failed. "Jesus, Son of David, have mercy on me!" Bartimaeus persisted, refusing to be quiet. This blind man saw more than many who could see!

"What do you want me to do for you?" Jesus asked the son of Timaeus. It was not an irrelevant or stupid question on Jesus' part. Bartimaeus had never been able to go to school. His only source of income was what he received from begging. He had learned no other trade. His blindness evoked sympathy from many who passed by, and as a sighted man he would be far less effective as a beggar. Especially at Passover time, pilgrims on their way to Jerusalem were particularly generous, thinking perhaps to earn a few extra brownie points from God for their gifts to the less fortunate. What *did* he really want Jesus to do for him?

Bartimaeus somehow knew that the words and touch of this rabbi were the words and touch of God. The mercy shown by this rabbi was the mercy of God. Should he receive healing, it would be a gift of God. How he would live, where he would go, what he would do next—those were questions of a secondary nature. "Jesus, Son of David, have mercy on me!" he cried out again.

And then—wonder of wonders—Jesus called for him! His cloak—his blanket by night and his only vestige of respectability by day—he tossed aside. He jumped to his feet and sensed the parting of the crowd that permitted him to go to the one whose calling had prompted his own.

"What do you want me to do for you?"

"Rabbi, I want to see."

Rabbi. Son of David. Messiah. I see!

Claim the Name

Jesus never forces any of us to see. Do you want to see him?

Having received his sight, Bartimaeus immediately got up and began to follow Jesus. Once we are able to see, following Jesus is what we are called to do.

> Open our eyes, Lord,
>   we want to see Jesus,
> To reach out and touch him,
>   and say that we love him.
> Open our ears, Lord,
>   and help us to listen.

*Open our eyes, Lord,
   we want to see Jesus. Amen.*

18

ZACCHAEUS

Jesus entered Jericho and was passing through. A man was there by the name of *Zacchaeus*; he was a chief tax collector and was wealthy. He wanted to see who Jesus was, but being a short man he could not, because of the crowd. So he ran ahead and climbed a sycamore-fig tree to see him, since Jesus was coming that way.

When Jesus reached the spot, he looked up and said to him, "*Zacchaeus*, come down immediately. I must stay at your house today."

So he came down at once and welcomed him gladly.

Luke 19:1–6

A sycamore-fig was a sturdy tree, thirty to forty feet high, with a short trunk, spreading branches, and large leaves. It could hold and perhaps hide a grown man, and it would not have been difficult to climb into its branches. This was the perch Zacchaeus chose to see the rabbi nearly everyone was talking about. No one was likely to favor him with the front row, which someone of his height would need in order to see, and though some in the crowd might whisper and mutter to each other *about* him, no one would have wanted to talk *with* him.

Zacchaeus was Jericho's chief IRS agent. As was the custom at the time, he could charge more tax than Rome required, keep the difference for himself, and rely on the power of the government to enforce whatever tariff he had asked. Zacchaeus was wealthy, greedy, and understandably unpopular.

We may not consider "receiving" to be one of the dimensions of gracious hospitality, but here Jesus demonstrates it in his interaction with Zacchaeus. Zacchaeus by his vocation and inclination has taken and taken and taken. He has never learned to give and doesn't know how to start. He has no friends with whom he might break bread and share his many other resources. He has stopped seeing those in need, like the blind Bartimaeus, who for years has waited hopefully just outside the Jericho gates.

As Jesus enters Jericho, he knows that the eternal tri-unity of God will be shattered during the week to come. The horror of this knowing surely weighed on him, and we could understand if Jesus had simply walked past the sycamore-fig tree, focused on what he soon had to do so that all humanity could be re-deemed. But no, it is Jesus' practice to see and call people one by one. What he will accomplish in the coming week is for the purpose of freeing Zacchaeus.

Today he will graciously and hospitably receive Zacchaeus' long-dormant hospitality.

The leafy sycamore-fig might have hidden Zacchaeus from the view of others, but Jesus sees him. Jesus stops and calls, "Zacchaeus, come down at once. I must stay at your house today."

Zacchaeus, I want to be your friend. Zacchaeus, I want to break bread with you. Zacchaeus, I have come to free you. For you, Zacchaeus, freedom will loosen your purse strings; it will open your heart.

Like muscles that have long lain in atrophy, Zacchaeus' hospitality and generosity begin to be stretched. He climbs down from the tree and welcomes Jesus gladly.

The crowd of proper people mutter in protest, but Zacchaeus doesn't care. As if to make up for lost time, he begins without delay to give half his possessions to those in need and to repay four times over those he has cheated. Jesus and Zacchaeus must have had a lovely dinner together that night! Who knows, maybe even Bartimaeus was invited.

Claim the Name

Has generosity lain dormant in your life? Do you wish that, like Zacchaeus, you could show hospitality to Jesus? Jesus himself tells of the day when he will say, "Whatever you did for one of the least of these brothers [and sisters] of mine, you did for me. . . . I was hungry and you gave me something to eat, I was thirsty and you gave me something to drink, I was a stranger and you invited me in, I needed clothes and you clothed me, I was sick and you looked after me, I was in prison and you came to visit me" (Matt. 25:40, 35–36).

> *What shall I render to the Lord for all his benefits to me?*
> *How shall my life, by grace restored, give worthy thanks, O Lord, to thee?*
>
> *With thankful heart I offer now my gift and call upon God's name.*
> *Before his saints I pay my vow and here my gratitude proclaim. Amen.*
>
> Psalm 116:12–19 versified for Psalter 1912, author unknown

19

HEIRS OF GOD

The Spirit himself testifies with our spirit that we are God's children. Now if we are children, then we are *heirs*—*heirs of God* and *co-heirs with Christ*, if indeed we share in his sufferings in order that we may also share in his glory.

Romans 8:16–17

"A will is in force only when somebody has died," the writer of Hebrews (9:17) reminds us. It takes a death for someone to become an heir. We are heirs of God because that is the will of Jesus, the somebody who has died. As with all beneficiaries of wills, the fact that we are God's heirs has everything to do with God's initiative and grace toward us. We have not earned or bought the benefits we have inherited, nor do we deserve them.

Present-day wills are ordinarily sealed by a notary; the seal serves to authenticate the will's directives. Jesus' will, as well, is sealed. The seal we have on his promises is the Holy Spirit. This is no phony document, for the Spirit authenticates this will.

What have we, God's heirs, inherited? We have received a name! We are no longer slaves; we are children of God (Gal. 4:7). We are co-heirs along with Jesus Christ. Charles, Anne, Harry, William—loyal British subjects know their surname even without its being mentioned. The British monarchy will likely be inherited by one of these four Windsors. But as children of God we can ask anything from the name that far surpasses that of earthly royalty, and God will hear and respond.

We all inherit physical and personality traits from the gene pool that has preceded us. He has Mom's curly red hair, she has Grandpa's dimple in her chin, he is talkative like Dad. Are there traits we inherit as children of God? If we are God's children, writes the apostle Paul in Romans 8:9, we will not be controlled by our sinful nature but by the Holy Spirit, who lives in us. We are made in God's image (Gen. 1:26–27). The traits we inherit as children of God may include our ability to love, our desire for another's highest good, our capacity to enjoy humor, our appreciation of beauty, and our power in certain circumstances to give names.

Present-day wills often mention material things— homes, businesses, jewelry, documents representing financial investments, even pets. We as God's heirs are promised that God will supply all our needs "according to his glorious riches in Christ Jesus" (Phil.

4:19). As the apostle Paul writes, we who are heirs will also "share in his [Christ's] sufferings in order that we may also share in his glory" (Rom. 8:17). What does that mean?

Christ's suffering has already been completed, and Christ's suffering is inextricably fused with Christ's glory. As far as we're concerned, it's as though we've inherited shares of stock in Christ's glory. But with those shares of glory-stock comes some residual suffering as a result of sin. It's part of the inheritance. The good news is that the suffering is temporary. Our glorious inheritance is life eternal—communion with God and the people of God in the kingdom of God forever!

Claim the Name

"See what great love the Father has lavished on us, that we should be called children of God! And that is what we are! The reason the world does not know us is that it did not know him. Dear friends, now we are children of God, and what we will be has not yet been made known. But we know that when Christ appears, we shall be like him, for we shall see him as he is. . . . For this is the message you heard from the beginning: We should love one another" (1 John 3:1–3, 11 TNIV).

> *Be thou my wisdom, and thou my true word,*
> *I ever with thee and thou with me, Lord;*
> *Thou my great Father, thy child shall I be,*
> *thou in me dwelling and I one with thee.*

Riches I heed not, nor vain empty praise,
    thou mine inheritance, now and always;
Thou and thou only, first in my heart,
    high King of heaven, my treasure thou art.
Amen.

Eleanor Hull, "Be Thou My Vision," 1912

20
THE BRIDE OF THE LAMB—
HER WEDDING CLOTHING

Hallelujah!
 For our Lord God Almighty reigns.
Let us rejoice and be glad
 and give him glory!
For the wedding of the Lamb has come,
 and his *bride* has made herself ready.
Fine linen, bright and clean,
 was given her to wear.
(Fine linen stands for the righteous acts of the saints.)

Revelation 19:6–8

Therefore, as God's chosen people, holy and dearly loved, clothe yourselves with compassion, kindness, humility, gentleness, and patience. Bear with each other and forgive whatever grievances you may have against one another. Forgive as the Lord forgave you. And over all these virtues put on love, which binds them all together in perfect unity.

Colossians 3:12–14

For many brides, few things occupy their attention more than what they will wear. Creativity, money, time, tradition, and a great deal of thought figure in the selection and preparation of the clothing worn on the wedding day.

As the Lamb's bride makes herself ready, fine linen, bright and clean, is given her to wear. The apostle John notes that the fine linen stands for the righteous acts of the saints. The apostle Paul describes this fine linen in more detail in Colossians 3: When the bride dons *compassion*, it becomes a lens through which she can view others to whom she can then reach out and serve with passion and fervor.

The bride clothed in *kindness* will appear beautiful no matter what else she wears, from the plainest to the most outrageous of clothing, for her kindness is evidence of her big heart. There is no meanness or arrogance in her.

The bride who clothes herself in *humility* has access to a true mirror—a very important asset when dressing. It allows her to see herself correctly, as God sees her. She is neither a doormat to be trampled on nor someone whose worth and beauty are the result of her own efforts.

No burlap or sackcloth for this bride's dress—nothing rough or scratchy. The fabric that wraps her is *gentleness*. This fabric invites the touch and feels good when worn. The quality attracts all who see her.

The bride clothed in *patience* knows that time is not the most important thing—her marriage will long outlast time. For her dress of patience she will not cut her time too short. She gifts time gladly, never grasping or protesting.

Bear with each other when dealing with other human beings might mean "put up with each other." But might it also mean "carry together"? When two have become one, a grievance that hurts one hurts both. Bear with, share whatever load the other is carrying. Do the things that grieve our Bridegroom also grieve us? Is it possible for us to share them?

The Bridegroom knows too how important it is for us to forgive the grievances we have with others. He both models for us and aids us in our forgiving. So then having been forgiven, *forgiveness* becomes as much a part of this bride's walk as the spring in her step.

Finally, that which coordinates the whole bridal outfit, tying it all together, is *love*. This bride loves because her Bridegroom first loved (1 John 4:19). What a trousseau she has!

But in the end it is not on her clothing that the bride focuses. Samuel Rutherford had it right when he wrote:

> The bride eyes not her garment, but her dear
>   Bridegroom's face;
> I will not gaze at glory but on my King of grace.
> Not at the crown he giveth but on his pierced
>   hand;
> The Lamb is all the glory of Immanuel's land.

VERSIFIED BY ANNE COUSIN, "THE SANDS OF TIME ARE SINKING," 1857

Claim the Name

We don't know when the marriage feast of the Lamb will take place, but we can begin to get dressed. Write the words *compassion, kindness, humility, gentleness, patience, bearing with each other, forgiveness,* and *love* on a small card and put it inside the door of the closet in which you keep your (other) clothing.

> *Holy Father of the Bride,*
> *Today we claim and clothe ourselves with the righteousness purchased at such great cost for us by our Bridegroom. Our hearts are filled with gratitude and praise. Amen.*

21

MY WITNESSES

But you will receive power when the Holy Spirit comes on you; and you will be *my witnesses* in Jerusalem, and in all Judea and Samaria, and to the ends of the earth.

Acts 1:8

She appeared flustered as she entered the room, juggling a large gift-wrapped box along with her jacket, umbrella, and handbag. None of the rest of the guests knew her. She looked around. "Is this 2429 Maplewood?" she asked.

"That's a block over from here," was the response.

"Oh! I'm so sorry! I guess I turned down the wrong street. I saw all the cars and thought this was the house I was looking for."

At that the catch on her handbag gave way, and all its contents spilled on the floor. She stooped and, with the help of several of the guests, replaced everything in her bag and went hastily on her way.

The host of the bridal shower then began passing out paper and pens. "How many of the items that were in my friend's bag can you name?" Some of the guests were better witnesses of what they had seen than others!

What makes a good witness? Someone who was there, of course. Someone who can say, "This is what I saw" or "That is what I heard" or "This is what I myself experienced." A good witness is someone who is attentive to details and can recall them accurately, as the shower guests would attest. A good witness is articulate and expresses her testimony clearly. A good witness is credible—perhaps someone whose past testimony has proven to be accurate or whose reputation and experience lend weight to his words.

We could be witnesses of any number of things, from spilled handbag contents, to a baby's first steps, to an automobile accident. Jesus said, "You will be *my* witnesses." Claiming that name was no easy thing for its first recipients. It is significant that the Greek word for witness is *martus*, the word from which we also derive our word *martyr*. Before the end of the first century, *witness* and *martyr* had merged into one word, for many of the witnesses Jesus first named did indeed become martyrs.

The apostle John is one of Jesus' trustworthy witnesses. In 1 John 1 he writes of Jesus, whose words he has heard personally. He writes of Jesus, whom he has seen with his own eyes and whom he has touched with his own hands. When he speaks of the eternal life Jesus has made possible for himself and for us, his words have the ring of truth.

What about us? Unlike the apostle John, we have never seen Jesus in the flesh. Most of us will not be put to death for our faith in Christ. Were Jesus' words, "You will be my witnesses," meant only for those assembled when he spoke them? Or are we meant to claim them?

The key here is in the preceding phrase: "You will receive power when the Holy Spirit comes on you." As twenty-first-century people of God, we have the Holy Spirit within us! It is the same Spirit whom Jesus promised his friends and whom they received on the day of Pentecost. That Spirit lives within us and empowers us both to see and to be the hand of God at work. We can witness to those times when we have seen God at work in our lives. We can tell our stories of God sightings, just as the apostle John did.

Perhaps we aren't seeing God in the circumstances that surround us today. We can't honestly claim the name witness. We need to ask ourselves the same question we ask when someone loses car keys: "When was the last time you remember having them?" When was the last time you remember that God was with you?

Joshua instructed the Israelites to make a pile of twelve stones, one for each tribe, to remind them of the way in which God had miraculously allowed them to cross the Jordan River on dry ground (Joshua 4). When the Israelites lost their bearings or forgot whose they were, the pile of stones could serve as a witness.

The Spirit who empowers us can point us back to our own pile of stones, to a time when we knew for sure that God was with us.

Being a witness can make us uncomfortable. Being a good witness is not always easy, as those shower guests discovered. Being a good witness can be terrifying, even life threatening. Being an effective witness of Jesus can happen only as we are empowered by his Spirit.

Claim the Name

Where is your "pile of stones"? How have you seen God at work in your own life? Write out your own story, simply and clearly, as you might tell it to a friend. Ask God to empower you to share that story with someone else.

> *Spirit of the Risen Jesus,*
> *Give substance to our witness by joining your witness to ours.*
> *Give life to our witness by being life in us.*
> *Give courage to our witness by granting us your power. Amen.*

ISHMAEL

Sarai treated Hagar so harshly that she finally ran away. The angel of the LORD found Hagar beside a spring of water in the wilderness, along the road to Shur. The angel said to her, "Hagar, Sarai's servant, where have you come from, and where are you going?"

"I'm running away from my mistress, Sarai," she replied.

The angel of the LORD said to her, "Return to your mistress, and submit to her authority." Then he added, "I will give you more descendants than you can count."

And the angel also said, "You are now pregnant and will give birth to a son. You are to name him *Ishmael* (which means 'God hears'), for the LORD has heard your cry of distress."

Genesis 16:6–11 NLT

Few "namings" in Scripture are clearer than this one. The angel of the Lord appears to Sarai's Egyptian slave, Hagar, and announces to her that she is pregnant with a son and is to name him Ishmael, "God hears." With this name, God offers a message to Hagar, to Abram and Sarai, to Ishmael himself, and to us.

That God hears does not mean God will always respond according to our timetable. God's promise that Abram's descendants would be as many as the stars had not found fruition quickly enough to suit Sarai. She had taken matters into her own hands, urging Abram to father a child by another woman.

That God hears does not prevent us from freely making choices, nor does it mean God will alter the course of history if we make poor choices. Centuries of conflict and bloodshed have flowed from that one decision made by Sarai and Abram.

But . . . God hears! Hagar's Creator is not so busy with other divine business that he turns a deaf or disinterested ear to her cries of distress. God hears! God does not sit back, impotent and unable to help. Hagar is led to shelter from the scorching sun and is shown water to cool herself and to drink.

That God hears does not mean God does things just the way we would choose to have them done! Returning to Sarai was *not* how Hagar saw her way forward. Yet that is what God tells her in no uncertain terms she must do.

God hears Sarai. God hears the ongoing unkindness of her words and treatment of Hagar. God hears Abram, whose unspoken words, had they been spoken, might perhaps have made a difference.

God hears Ishmael, even when perhaps Ishmael might have wished otherwise. God hears the times Ishmael quarrels with and plays mean tricks on his younger brother. God hears but does not prevent the animosity of two mothers from continuing in their children. God hears Abram's prayer on Ishmael's behalf and will make him the fruitful father of a great people. Ishmael—"God hears." It is both a warning and a blessing.

We too are Ishmael, for God hears us as well. The God who hears us walks with us, even when we choose the wrong path. In and through and with all our choices, our hearing God is at work.

The God who hears "slumbers not, nor sleeps"— he hears us all the time. It is not the listening of a distracted parent who mutters, "Uh huh," but whose attention is far away on other matters. The God who hears us stoops to our level and listens intently to our petitions. God always responds. Reminders of who God is are sometimes the response we receive.

Claim the Name

God hears! That might make you thankful, or it might make you squeamish; for twenty-first-century Ishmaels as well, this name is both a blessing and a warning.

Today consider what God is hearing from you. Like Ishmael you can choose what that will be.

> *God Who Hears,*
> *May the words of our mouths and the thoughts*
> *of our hearts be pleasing to your ears, O Lord,*
> *our strength and our Redeemer! Amen.*

SAMUEL

Then Eli realized that the LORD was calling the boy. So Eli told Samuel, "Go and lie down, and if he calls you, say, 'Speak, LORD, for your servant is listening.'" So Samuel went and lay down in his place.

The LORD came and stood there, calling as at the other times, *"Samuel! Samuel!"*

Then Samuel said, "Speak, for your servant is listening." . . .

The LORD was with Samuel as he grew up, and he let none of his words fall to the ground. And all Israel from Dan to Beersheba recognized that Samuel was attested as a prophet of the LORD. The LORD continued to appear at Shiloh, and there he revealed himself to Samuel through his word. And Samuel's word came to all Israel.

1 Samuel 3:8–10, 19–21

It is difficult to imagine even a godly and grateful twenty-first-century mother entrusting the upbringing of her just-weaned, only child to an elderly priest whose parenting credentials were at least suspect. Yet that is what Samuel's mother, Hannah, and father, Elkanah, did. Samuel was taken to the city of Shiloh, where the ark of God was located, making it the central place of worship for the people of God. Samuel was given to God and placed in the care of the priest Eli.

Communication from God had been rare in those days (1 Sam. 3:1). But Eli at least recognized that the voice Samuel was hearing had to be God's. He did not hoard the divine communication, thinking that if anyone were to hear from God, he himself would have been a more worthy audience than his young protégé. Eli instructed Samuel on how to listen and how to respond. And Samuel did as he was told.

The God to whom we respond listens to and hears us. How well do we listen for God? Would we, like Samuel initially, fail to recognize the voice of God? Are our lives so full of noise that God's voice is drowned out? What would we do with a difficult message? How might God speak to us today?

As Samuel grew up, he and God continued to fellowship together. Samuel "let none of his [God's] words fall to the ground" (1 Sam. 3:19). Do we cup our hands tightly to prevent any of the precious jewels—words of God poured out to us—from falling out? Or are some of God's words to us lost, others ignored, and still others disobeyed? The first words God entrusted to Samuel were a severe prophecy for Eli and his family. Not an easy message to deliver, but Samuel delivered it. Throughout Samuel's life he proved to be a faithful conduit for the words of the Lord. And all Israel recognized it.

Perhaps you have played the party game "Telephone." Someone whispers a message into the ear of the next person, who in turn whispers it to the next person, and so on until the message has gone around the circle. Nearly always the original message is garbled. Could God rely on us to pass his words on to others? Would we do it in a timely and accurate way? Speak, Lord, for your servant is listening!

Claim the Name

Who has been a Samuel in passing God's word on to you? Are you actively listening for God's voice? Is there someone with whom you should share God's word?

> *Lord, speak to me that I may speak in living echoes*
> *of your tone.*
> *As you have sought, so let me seek your erring*
> *children lost and lone.*
>
> *O use me, Lord, use even me, just as you will, and*
> *when, and where*
> *Until your blessed face I see, your rest, your joy,*
> *your glory share. Amen.*

Frances Ridley Havergal, "Lord, Speak to Me," 1872

24

THE APPLE OF GOD'S EYE

For the Lᴏʀᴅ's portion is his people,
  Jacob his allotted inheritance.
In a desert land he found him, . . .
  he guarded him as *the apple of his eye*.
                              Deuteronomy 32:9–10

I call on you, O God, for you will answer me;
  give ear to me and hear my prayer.
Show the wonder of your great love,
  you who save by your right hand
  those who take refuge in you from their foes.
Keep me as *the apple of your eye*;
  hide me in the shadow of your wings.
                                    Psalm 17:6–8

The apple of the eye is the pupil, delicate and highly vulnerable. Without it we could not see, and since seeing is so important to the body, the apple is protected and cared for at all costs. The Creator at the outset provided some built-in "apple guards." Our eyelids and eyelashes close protectively even without our thinking about them. Even unbidden, our tears wash out foreign objects that might harm the apple. Probably because of the high value we place on functioning eyesight, the metaphor "the apple of the eye" came to mean something or someone that is cherished.

We are vulnerable—yet deemed important enough to be protected and cared for. And the one who protects and cares for us does it not simply out of duty but out of love. We are cherished! People of God, we are the apple of God's eye!

It was to have been simply a routine check of our furnace and heating system, but a highly attentive inspector discovered major gas leaks from the pipe buried under the concrete floor of our garage that carried gas into our home. My white-faced furnace inspector summoned me to the garage. There I too could hear the gas-leak detecting device ticking wildly, indicating the presence of escaping gas. "One spark! That's all it would have taken!" he exclaimed quietly. We are the apple of God's eye. The one who created us actively watches over us, protecting us when we know we need it and even when we are unaware of our need.

When the extended family gathered for Thanksgiving Day dinner, we took a piece of what had been our gas pipe, rusty and with obvious holes, and made of it a centerpiece for our dinner table. It was for us a reminder to give thanks.

The designation "apple of God's eye" suggests the extent to which God cares for us. This name can serve as a mirror. As we peer into it, we can see, perhaps to our amazement, a reflection of how God sees us. We have truly been shown the wonder of God's great love! How can it be that we have the value to God that the pupil of the eye has to the body? How can we possibly respond?

Cherished child of God, apple of God's eye, give thanks today for the ways God protects and cares for you. Praise him with all you are and all you do.

Claim the Name

Cherished child of God, apple of God's eye, how have *you* seen God's protection and care for you demonstrated? Spend some time reflecting and recalling. Share your story with someone else.

> *I call upon you, O God, for you will answer me;*
> *give ear to me and hear my prayer.*
> *Show the wonder of your great love,*
> *you who save by your right hand*
> *those who take refuge in you from their foes.*
> *Keep me as the apple of your eye;*
> *hide me in the shadow of your wings. Amen.*

> Psalm 17:6–8

25

SINNERS

But God demonstrates his own love for us in this: While we were still *sinners*, Christ died for us.

Romans 5:8

Sinners. Must we accept this name? Surely there are so many people more deserving of it than we are!

How little we know ourselves, and how quickly we skip to the end of the story. How readily we sing with Charles Wesley, "Hark! The herald angels sing, 'Glory to the newborn King; peace on earth and mercy mild, God and sinners reconciled!'"

In *The Beatitudes and the Lord's Prayer for Everyman*, William Barclay traces an interesting progression in the apostle Paul's own spiritual awareness. In the first words of Paul's earliest epistle, Galatians, which he wrote about AD 48, he refers to himself as "Paul, an apostle" (1:1). Seven years later (AD 55) he wrote to the Corinthians saying, "I am the least of the apostles and do not even deserve to be called an apostle" (1 Cor. 15:9). To the Ephesians in about AD 63 Paul wrote, "I am less than the least of all God's people" (3:8). As Paul awaited his death, he wrote to Timothy, "Christ Jesus came into the world to save sinners—of whom I am the worst" (1 Tim. 1:15). Paul's experience parallels all of ours: The closer we get to the holy God, the more clearly we see the magnitude of our own sin.

But Paul knew, and we can know, that his story didn't end with the magnitude of his own sin. His story ends with Paul, sinner, clothed in Christ's righteousness.

Seeing her in the first place had happened innocently enough. She was gorgeous. And her husband was away. Desire simmered within David until it rose to a full boil. He wanted her desperately. David, man after God's own heart, sinned grievously. David, man after God's own heart, acknowledged his sin and cried out to God for mercy and cleansing. David, sinner, clothed in Christ's righteousness.

Could Isaiah feel the burning from that live coal afterward? Did it leave a mark others could see? Had it been easy for him before to go through worship motions, to repeat worship words? Many of us know what that is like. But then Isaiah saw the holy, holy, holy, Lord Almighty! The whole place shook and filled with smoke. Isaiah saw himself with new eyes. He cried out to God for mercy. Isaiah, sinner, clothed in Christ's righteousness.

Sinners. Yes, it's a name we must accept, along with Paul, David, and Isaiah. But it's a name that Jesus has forever changed. Mary—you may insert your own name—sinner, clothed in Christ's righteousness. Charles Wesley was right; God and sinners are reconciled!

Claim the Name

"If we confess our sins, he [God] is faithful and just and will forgive us our sins and purify us from all unrighteousness. If we claim we have not sinned, we make him out to be a liar and his word has no place in our lives" (1 John 1:9–10).

Christ Jesus,

You came into the world to save sinners—of whom I am the worst. But for that very reason I was shown mercy so that in me, the worst of sinners, you might display your unlimited patience as an example for those who would believe on you and receive eternal life.

Now to the King eternal, immortal, invisible, the only God, be honor and glory for ever and ever. Amen.

1 Timothy 1:15–17, adapted

26

PRIESTS

You will be for me a kingdom of *priests* and a holy
nation.

Exodus 19:6

You also . . . are being built into a spiritual house to be a
holy priesthood, offering spiritual sacrifices acceptable
to God through Jesus Christ.

1 Peter 2:5

What an honor it was for the newly freed
Israelites to be called by God a "kingdom
of priests"! As slaves in Egypt, none of
them could have been a priest. It would be through
this kingdom of priests that one would come who
could serve as the once-for-all mediator between
God and humankind. Early on, the Israelites were

instructed to set aside one tribe, the Levites, to serve as priests for them all. Those priests of long ago and the unblemished animals they offered as sacrifices were object lessons pointing to the coming of a great High Priest (Heb. 4:14–16). Jesus' perfect sacrifice for us all eliminated the need for those animal object lessons, but the work of the priest could not continue apart from his sacrifice. That sacrifice expanded the priesthood so that the apostle Peter could refer to his readers as a "holy priesthood."

A priest is a mediary agent between humans and God. We bring to our calling of priest different pictures, depending on our general experience as well as that particular to our corporate worship. It is important to remember that even though we are priests, this doesn't mean we don't need a priest! For the work of the priest is intercessory prayer, for oneself as well as for others.

This serving as a mediary agent is hard work. Often the work is not highly visible. Sometimes it may not be properly appreciated. The one who brings two live wires together is all but forgotten when the sparks begin to fly and the power begins to flow. The intercessor, who by definition bridges the gap between God and his people, becomes one with those prayed for, lifting Godward their doubts, sins, questions, and concerns. Those prayed for may be too weak or perhaps too proud to pray for themselves. This is heavy lifting! It is one of the most important things the people of God do for one another. There are times when our own grief and pain weigh so heavily we can't pray properly. We need the prayers of others in the holy priesthood to lift our neediness to God's

throne of grace. There are other times when we ourselves have the honor of interceding as priests through
Jesus Christ.

And when all our human intercession fails, "the
Spirit helps us in our weakness. [When] we do not
know what we ought to pray [for], . . . the Spirit himself intercedes for us with groans that words cannot
express . . . in accordance with God's will" (Rom.
8:26–27).

Claim the Name

Perhaps today you need a priest—someone to lift your
needs and concerns to God. Ask God to show you
whom you could ask to serve as a priest for you.

Perhaps today you are to serve as a priest for someone else, both to intercede in prayer on their behalf
and then to speak God's words of grace to them. Ask
God to show you who this is.

> *Lord, listen to your children praying,*
>   *Lord, send your Spirit in this place;*
>   *Lord, listen to your children praying,*
>   *Send us love, send us power, send us grace.*
> *Amen.*

27

MARY OF MAGDALA

"Woman," he said, "why are you crying? Who is it you are looking for?"

Thinking he was the gardener, she said, "Sir, if you have carried him away, tell me where you have put him, and I will get him."

Jesus said to her, "*Mary*."

John 20:15–16

There were times she couldn't even scratch an itch if the demon spirits inhabiting her body capriciously prevented her from doing so. There were seven of them, nameless spirits known to her only by their numbers. It seemed they never slept—so she rarely could. They dictated all utterances of their unwilling host, punctuating them with diabolical shrieks. She could do nothing but at their bidding. A captivity of greater horror would be hard to imagine.

Then one day she encountered someone who had access to greater power than that of demons. At his command the exorcised evil spirits fled, and she was free (Luke 8:2)!

In this text Mary of Magdala is weeping outside the tomb of the one she has followed since he freed her to be the woman she was meant to be. She stooped as she did so to look inside. Through her tears she saw two white-clothed beings seated where Jesus' body had been laid. "Why are you weeping?" they asked. Why wouldn't she be weeping? How could they not realize? Their query only drew from her more tears.

She turned and saw someone else standing near the tomb who asked the same seemingly senseless questions. "Why are you weeping? Who is it you are looking for?"

"Sir," she blurted, thinking perhaps he was the gardener, "if you have carried him away, tell me where you have put him, and I will get him."

Jesus said to her, "Mary."

Jesus called her by her *name*, not by her gender— woman. Not by the town from which she came— Magdala. Not by some occupation such as seller of purple or seamstress. Not by an expression of her relationship to someone else—daughter of . . . wife of . . . mother of . . . Jesus said to her simply, "Mary."

With the hearing of her name came comprehension. Hope. Joy.

"Teacher!" she cried.

"Go tell the others what you have seen."

As with Mary of Magdala, we owe much to the one who names us. As with Mary, God sees more than the place we were born, more than our gender, more than our vocation or avocations, and more than those to whom we are related. God sees you and me—who we truly are.

Perhaps like Mary we are absorbed by the seemingly hopeless circumstances in which we find ourselves. Perhaps we too can barely see Jesus through our tears. Like Mary we must stop and listen. Do you hear your name?

Claim the Name

Even if your name isn't Mary, the Lord has said, "I have called you by name; you are mine" (Isa. 43:1). Today look to see who it is that calls *you* by name. Mary responded by exclaiming her name for Jesus, "Teacher!" Which of Jesus' names is particularly meaningful for you today?

Jesus tells Mary to tell the others what she has seen. You are invited to do the same.

> *Risen Lord Jesus,*
>   *You have named us, and in that naming we have seen who you are.*
>   *Today we want to follow you and tell others what we have seen, as Mary did. Amen.*

28

JACOB—RENAMED ISRAEL

So Jacob was left alone, and a man wrestled with him till daybreak. When the man saw that he could not overpower him, he touched the socket of Jacob's hip so that his hip was wrenched as he wrestled with the man. Then the man said, "Let me go, for it is daybreak."

But Jacob replied, "I will not let you go unless you bless me."

The man asked him, "What is your name?"

"Jacob," he answered.

Then the man said, "Your name will no longer be *Jacob*, but *Israel*, because you have struggled with God and with men and have overcome."

Genesis 32:24–28

An intercollegiate wrestling match lasts a total of eight minutes, divided into three periods of two, three, and three minutes. To succeed in pinning the shoulders of the opponent in the allotted eight minutes, a wrestler must be strong, fast, coordinated, in good physical shape, and have a knowledge of body leverage. It is difficult to imagine a wrestling match that could go on all night, in the dark!

Jacob had been a wrestler of sorts since he was in utero, where he and his twin brother, Esau, jostled with each other (Gen. 25:22). He exited his mother's womb with his hand grasping his slightly older brother's heel. By conniving with his mother, tricking his father, Isaac, and tempting his brother, he grasped for himself both the birthright inheritance and the blessing that traditionally would have gone to the elder Esau.

After fleeing from his brother's wrath, Jacob nearly met his match in the person of his uncle Laban, who was almost as conniving as Jacob. Laban squeezed out fourteen instead of the agreed-upon seven years of labor in exchange for marriage to Laban's second daughter, Rachel. The time finally came for Jacob to return to his childhood home. Jacob managed to manipulate things so he could claim an inordinately large portion of the flocks he had cared for as his share. With the animals, his wives, children, and servants, he set out for home.

The night before the inevitable encounter with Esau, Jacob sent his entire entourage, everyone and everything, across the river Jabbok. He remained alone. He had much to think about. Perhaps he did some praying—Scripture makes no mention of Jacob praying or worshiping Yahweh since the time he fled from Esau many years earlier (Genesis 28).

In the dark of night, Jacob's solitude was interrupted by someone with whom he began to wrestle. (In the Near East, legal cases were sometimes settled by an ordeal, or test, and wrestling was one mode used.) At some point Jacob realized with whom he was wrestling. His adversary was equipping him with the extraordinary strength and stamina he needed to continue! Near daybreak the opponent proposed they call it a draw. But Jacob's objective was to receive God's blessing, and he insisted.

God's blessing would be God's approval, God's yes on Jacob. Jacob had longed for that approval in his youth, and he longed for it now. He knew his own sinfulness and his need to be made right with God. He was apprehensive about a future without God's yes on his life. So *Elohim Shaddai*, the night wrestler, responded by touching or striking Jacob in such a way that his hip was dislocated. The thigh was thought to be the seat of reproductive power. A descendant of Jacob would, like Jacob, be struck (Isa. 53:4) and would overcome. For Jacob to find approval from God, to be blessed, it would take the work of this descendant Jesus—the very one with whom he was wrestling! In addition to the blessing, Jacob received a new name, Israel, which means to strive or wrestle with God.

Israel has many descendants who, like him, wrestle with God. Many, like him, come to a realization of the one with whom they wrestle. All the striving and wrestling we do to gain God's approval is for nothing unless we acknowledge and receive the strength and the righteousness made available to us through Jacob's descendant, the night wrestler.

Claim the Name

Jacob is not condemned for wrestling with God. He is sustained and strengthened as he wrestles by the very one who has earned for him the approval and blessing he strives for. God's yes can be ours as well, because of Jesus.

> Did we in our own strength confide, our striving
> would be losing,
> Were not the right Man on our side, the Man of
> God's own choosing.
> You ask who that may be? Christ Jesus, it is he;
> Lord Sabaoth his name,
> From age to age the same; and he must win the
> battle. Amen.

Martin Luther, "A Mighty Fortress," 1529

29

LIGHT

You're here to be *light*, bringing out the God-colors in the world. God is not a secret to be kept. We're going public with this, as public as a city on a hill. If I make you light-bearers, you don't think I'm going to hide you under a bucket, do you? I'm putting you on a light stand. Now that I've put you there on a hilltop, on a light stand—shine! Keep open house; be generous with your lives. By opening up to others, you'll prompt people to open up with God, this generous Father in heaven.

Matthew 5:14–16 Message

Light is one of our Bridegroom's names, gifted to us. Jesus said, "While I am in the world, I am the light of the world" (John 9:5). But this same Jesus also said, "You're here to be light." Presumptuous though it may feel to claim this powerful God-name for ourselves, being bearers of God-light is a task delegated particularly to those of us who live after Jesus' bodily return to heaven.

Before we start to feel too inadequate, we need to remember that this business of being light is not really about *us*. It is about Jesus Christ. Like a moon or a mirror, our job is to reflect the light. Are there smudges on our lives that distort the light of Christ? Are we wrapped in clouds that block it?

Sometimes light rays are absorbed, as sunlight on a black rooftop or a flashlight underneath blankets. It doesn't make sense to light a lamp only to hide it, as Jesus noted. God, having made us light-bearers, surely won't quench that light, even if we sometimes think we have good reason to hide it, perhaps using it to read, all alone, under our bed covers! But Jesus makes it clear that God intends for God-light to be shared.

The God-light we reflect exposes evil. Sometimes its piercing laser beam can surgically remove a malignancy, allowing healing to take place. This light is meant to clarify truth. Eyes are useless and seeing is incomprehensible without light. And nothing can grow without light; God-light is meant to facilitate the growth that needs to take place around us.

When we who are accustomed to artificial lighting experience a power outage, we often light a candle when we enter a darkened room. Even that one candle makes a difference in what we can see. But Jesus didn't delegate this task of being light only to a single individual. Being light is meant to be a group effort. When the first astronauts circled the earth, entire cities turned on their lights as the space capsule passed over them, as a salute to the orbiting men. This great concert of lights accomplished what one light alone would have been insufficient to do.

Even though people of God sometimes feel like solitary candles shedding light that is limited and ineffectual, the reality is that the light of Christ, refracted through the church's prism, shines forth in waves of every length, creating every shade of red, orange, yellow, green, blue, and violet. We're here together to be light, bringing out the God-colors in the world!

Claim the Name

Think about some of the aspects of light as they relate to your life. Perhaps today something you say or do will help someone near you to grow. Perhaps you will help another person to see more clearly. Perhaps today you will join your light to that of others, helping to form a brilliant light concert to the praise of God. Today God names you light. Where and how will you shine?

Lord Jesus, our Light,

We are humbled at this task to which you have called us.

Forgive us for wanting to crawl under the nearest bushel basket.

Forgive us for believing you have no place to use our light.

Forgive us for thinking that being light is about us and only us.

Wash away the smudges that keep us from reflecting truly.

Fuel us so that we can shine until you come again. Amen.

30
SHEEP

We are his people, the *sheep* of his pasture.

Psalm 100:3

We all, like *sheep*, have gone astray,
each of us has turned to his own way.

Isaiah 53:6

He calls his own *sheep* by name and leads them out.
. . . My *sheep* listen to my voice; I know them, and they
follow me. I give them eternal life, and they shall never
perish; no one can snatch them out of my hand.

John 10:3, 27–28

Sheep were familiar creatures to those who wrote
down the words of Scripture as well as to Scripture's first recipients. The people of God are

referred to in Scripture as sheep or lambs more often than by any other name.

In England's Cotswold country, hikers are welcome to walk across privately owned fields and pastures. But it doesn't take much for the sheep in a pasture to panic and quickly scatter to its far corners. A hiker can easily manipulate the sheep gates that separate pastures, but a sheep requires human pushing and prodding to pass through those gates. Sheep are not known for their high degree of intelligence.

When a sheep is heavy with wool, it is easy for it to become cast—on its back with its feet in the air. When this happens, the sheep is helpless to regain its footing without human assistance, and it will soon die, as blood circulation is cut off in this position.

Lost sheep are unable to find their own way home. Sheep, if left on their own, will follow the same trails until they create ruts and will graze in exactly the same places until those grazing spots become polluted and barren. Sheep are truly dependent on their shepherd for nourishment and water. A lost sheep, if not soon found, will die.

Sheep are prey to many predators and when confronted are essentially helpless, incapable of acting in their own defense. David tells King Saul how he killed lions and bears in the course of caring for his sheep (1 Sam. 17:34–35). A sheep is dependent on the shepherd for protection.

Few animals are less able to deal with pests that exasperate them, such as ticks and flies. For this too sheep depend on the shepherd.

And there is a "butting order" among sheep! Rivalry, bullying, jealousy, and tension can occur within a flock of sheep. The presence of the shepherd is the most effective means of diffusing this tension.

No wonder, then, a sheep learns its life depends on the shepherd. No wonder a sheep learns to know the sound of the shepherd's voice. The shepherd represents protection and nourishment. A sheep, unable to lie down and rest unless it is free from hunger, fear, pests, and bullies, can do so with confidence when the shepherd is near.

Sheep—perhaps not the name we'd choose for ourselves—are easily scattered, easily rendered helpless, easily bullied, neither very smart nor very fast. But we are sheep well cared for. Our shepherd calls us by name. We have been given eternal life. We will never perish. No one—*no one*—can snatch us out of the shepherd's hand!

Claim the Name

Read John 10:1–18. What characteristic of a sheep do you most relate to? Why? Jesus says that his sheep listen to his voice and follow him (John 10:27). How can you do a better job of listening? Of following?

> You, LORD, are my shepherd, I shall not be in
> want.
> You make me lie down in green pastures, you lead
> me beside quiet waters;
> You restore my soul.
> You guide me in paths of righteousness for your
> name's sake.
> Even though I walk through the valley of the

*shadow of death, I will fear no evil, for you
are with me;*
Your rod and your staff, they comfort me.
*You prepare a table before me in the presence of
my enemies.*
You anoint my head with oil; my cup overflows.
*Surely goodness and love will follow me all the
days of my life;*
*And I will dwell in the house of the LORD forever.
Amen.*

Psalm 23, adapted

31
SHEPHERDS

Be *shepherds* of God's flock that is under your care, serving as overseers—not because you must, but because you are willing, as God wants you to be; not greedy for money, but eager to serve; not lording it over those entrusted to you, but being examples to the flock. And when the Chief Shepherd appears, you will receive the crown of glory that will never fade away.

1 Peter 5:2–4

Keep watch over yourselves and all the flock of which the Holy Spirit has made you overseers. Be *shepherds* of the church of God, which he bought with his own blood.

Acts 20:28

In Phillip Keller's *A Shepherd Looks at the Good Shepherd and His Sheep*, he tells the story of a slightly built Masai shepherd, only about ten years old, who had been given sole responsibility for his family's flock. A young lioness approached and dared to attack one of his sheep. No one stronger or more experienced was around, so he took on the lioness himself. Single-handedly he speared and managed to kill the lioness, but not without being severely injured and nearly losing his own life. But these were his sheep! He knew their names. He loved them and cared for them. Not one of them would be lost. Not on his watch.

The above Scripture passages are often used during installation services for church office-bearers. But for most of us there are seasons, or contexts, in which we are called on to be shepherds over a portion of God's people. Being a good shepherd consumes an enormous amount of time, it is not glamorous, it is sometimes lonely, and it is sometimes dangerous. It is an especially daunting task because we know the Chief Shepherd, and we know how far short we fall by comparison. But today, like the young Masai, we're the ones on watch.

We can learn much about shepherding if we keep our eyes focused on the Chief Shepherd. The Chief Shepherd *loves* his sheep. He does not see their care as a duty. We are to shepherd joyfully and willingly, never grudgingly, out of guilt, or because seven other people turned down the job. We invite those in our care to follow us, as we ourselves closely follow the Chief Shepherd (1 Cor. 11:1). We are to be examples, but we must get out of the way if by following us the sheep are going astray. Human shepherds must be ever mindful that this is *God's* flock. Our job is always to nudge the sheep Godward.

We should not consider serving as an under-shepherd for its profitability. Being a shepherd may involve personal sacrifice, as it did for the young Masai. Sheep are not known for being mindful of the shepherd's feelings, nor are they known for expressing appreciation.

Shepherds must keep their eyes open—they are told to keep watch and are referred to as overseers. Shepherds need to be mindful of dangers that lurk perhaps unseen, as well as of dangers that do not at the outset appear dangerous. Paul, mindful that the Ephesian "shepherds" to whom he is speaking are themselves "sheep" as well, urges them to "keep watch over yourselves" (Acts 20:28).

So why be a shepherd? First, because the Chief Shepherd has given us sheep to care for and has called us to the task. Second, when the Chief Shepherd appears, the flock that has been kept and cared for will bring him glory forever. As under-shepherds we will share that glory!

Claim the Name

Shepherds, take care of yourselves. When preflight instructions are given concerning the possible use of oxygen masks during the flight, passengers are told to put their own masks in place before attempting to assist a child or someone else in need of help. If you as a shepherd are not getting what you need, you are not likely to be able to help someone else. Are you being nourished? Does your own soul need to be restored? Keep watch over yourselves too!

The apostle Peter urges all of us to clothe ourselves with humility. We are to humble ourselves so that God may lift us up. We shepherds can cast all our anxiety on our Chief Shepherd, because he cares for us (from 1 Peter 5:5–7).

> *May the God of peace, who through the blood of the eternal covenant brought back from the dead our Lord Jesus, that great Shepherd of the sheep, equip you with everything good for doing his will, and may he work in us what is pleasing to him, through Jesus Christ, to whom be glory for ever and ever. Amen.*
>
> Hebrews 13:20–21

32

SAUL, ALSO CALLED PAUL

Meanwhile, *Saul* was still breathing out murderous threats against the Lord's disciples. He went to the high priest and asked him for letters to the synagogues in Damascus, so that if he found any there who belonged to the Way, whether men or women, he might take them as prisoners to Jerusalem. As he neared Damascus on his journey, suddenly a light from heaven flashed around him. He fell to the ground and heard a voice say to him, "*Saul, Saul*, why do you persecute me?"

"Who are you, Lord?" *Saul* asked.

"I am Jesus, whom you are persecuting," he replied. "Now get up and go into the city, and you will be told what you must do."

Acts 9:1–6

While they were worshiping the Lord and fasting, the Holy Spirit said, "Set apart for me Barnabas and *Saul* for the work to which I have called them." . . . Then

Saul, who was also called *Paul*, filled with the Holy Spirit, looked straight at Elymas.

Acts 13:2, 9

aul. This Hebrew name means "prayed for." If we ever doubt the effectiveness of prayer, we would do well to consider Saul!

Most Hebrew males acquired their father's name as part of their own; Simon Peter bar Jonas, and James and John bar Zebedee are examples. But we are not told Saul's father's name; what we know of him we must infer from the name given to his son: "prayed for."

Who was it that prayed for Saul? We can imagine Saul's parents praying for him, even before he was born, and they surely prayed for him all the years he was growing up. More remarkable is Stephen (Acts 9), who, as he was being stoned to death, prayed that God would not hold this sin against Saul and the others responsible. Jesus had instructed his followers to pray for those who did evil to them. So it is possible that other followers of Jesus also prayed for this man, even as with great zeal he lashed out, intent on destroying them.

We know that Jesus intercedes for all of us twenty-first-century Sauls, as he surely did for this first-century one. It was "Saul, Saul"—the prayed-for one—to whom Jesus called out as, accompanied by blazing light, he spoke directly from heaven.

Ananias, a follower of Jesus, showed hospitality—no doubt with some trepidation—and prayed for Saul. The Spirit of Jesus then came to Saul, filled him, and his life was reoriented 180 degrees!

Saul, in addition to being a devout Jew, was also a bona fide citizen of Rome, having been born in the Roman city of Tarsus. So he also had the Greco-Roman name of Paul. We can imagine a mother cuddling her precious newborn in the curve of her arm and thinking, "Paulus," just the perfect name for this little one! At the end of his life, the apostle used the name Paul exclusively. We don't know exactly when Saul began to use the name Paul, and we don't know with certainty why. It is possible that God renamed him, as Jesus claimed the name Peter for Simon, but Scripture doesn't say. It is also possible that Saul himself elected to use his Gentile name when it became clear that he was to be God's witness primarily to the Gentiles, those people who were not Jews.

But in addition, Saul may have chosen to use the name Paul because of its meaning, for to the new Paul it would have made a delightful pun. The name Paul in Greek means "little" or "less." No longer is he stridently confident of his own importance, sure of his own rightness! It would be like this changed man to want us to remember "little" or "less" about him and to focus our attention on what he had to say about Jesus and what Jesus had done for him. Paul would have us join the Roman believers in offering "to the only wise God . . . glory forever through Jesus Christ! Amen" (Rom. 16:27).

Claim the Name

Give thanks that like Saul you are prayed for! Then like Paul abandon your own rightness and claim instead the righteousness of Jesus that God has offered to us.

With the apostle Paul, and in the words of John the Baptist, we can decide, "He must become greater; I must become less" (John 3:30).

> *My gracious Master and my God, assist me to proclaim,*
> *To spread through all the earth abroad the honors of your name. Amen.*

Charles Wesley, "O for a Thousand Tongues to Sing," 1739

33

MERCIFUL

Blessed are the *merciful* [*eleos*],
   for they will be shown mercy.

Matthew 5:7

He has shown all you people what is good.
   And what does the LORD require of you?
   To act justly and to love *mercy* [*hesed*]
   and to walk humbly with your God.

Micah 6:8 TNIV

Then Naomi said to her two daughters-in-law, "Go back, each of you, to your mother's home. May the LORD show kindness [*hesed*] to you, as you have shown to your dead and to me."

Ruth 1:8

"The LORD bless him!" Naomi said to her daughter-in-law. "The LORD has not stopped showing his kindness [*hesed*] to the living and the dead."

Ruth 2:20

"The LORD bless you, my daughter," he replied. "This kindness [*hesed*] is greater than that which you showed earlier."

Ruth 3:10

Wherever we look in the pages of Scripture, we are confronted with the mercy of God, for mercy is the grand theme of the Bible. The Hebrew word *hesed* used in the Old Testament becomes the Greek word *eleos* used in the New. Most of the time the word is used of God, and if we were allowed only one word to describe Yahweh God and his relationship to us, we would do well to choose "merciful." No wonder then that the initiator and demonstrator of mercy calls on kingdom citizens to be merciful.

Our English translations fail to unpack the richness of the original word. *Hesed* keepers are characterized by faithfulness, sacrificial courage, and true lovingkindness. *Hesed* is a word often associated with God's covenant, to show the kind and loyal attitude each party ought to have toward the other.

In the book of Ruth we have a beautiful picture of merciful (*hesed*) relationships. We struggle sometimes to understand how God can be sovereign and at the same time we as humans are free to choose. In this composition of *hesed* relationships we see a harmony created with these two seemingly clashing melodies.

Even though Naomi urged her to do otherwise, Ruth courageously chose to accompany her mother-in-law to a new and foreign country and an unknowable future. After arriving in Bethlehem, Ruth "went out and began to glean. . . . As it turned out, she found herself working in a field belonging to Boaz" (Ruth 2:3). No angel came to her in a dream with instructions, as happened with the magi, Zechariah, Joseph, and Mary. No one made her go. No one told her which field to enter. Yet throughout this entire story there can be no doubt that God's firm, guiding hand is at work. It is true that with great care the sovereign God put in place each branch of Jesus' family tree. It is no less true that Ruth "happened" to glean in Boaz' field. The human kindness shown is seen by the other characters in the story as God's kindness, for when we are merciful we are demonstrating God's mercy.

Long before Jesus spoke his blessing on merciful kingdom citizens, the prophet Micah reminded Israel that *hesed*, this intertwining and aligning of human and divine behavior (mercy), is what the Lord requires. About seven hundred years later when the disciples ask Jesus how they should pray, the model Jesus gives them includes the petition, "Your [God's] will be done on earth as it is in heaven" (Matt. 6:10). What are we really asking God for when we pray these words? Heaven wouldn't be heaven if the sovereign God's will didn't happen there.

But on earth—for a reason difficult for us to comprehend—God created humans who are free to choose. Humans like Orpah (Ruth 1:14), who can choose to go back to Moab. Humans like the nearer kinsman (Ruth 4:6), who can choose to pass up the opportunity to act as a redeemer. And humans like Ruth and Boaz, who with courage and compassion can choose to respond to God's call to be merciful. Such humans pray that their choices and their very lives will further God's will on earth, as it is in heaven— for that is what mercy looks like. Blessed are those to whom and through whom God's mercy pours; they are the ongoing recipients of it.

Claim the Name

To be merciful is to be and to act as God would, for God is merciful. Even without personal instructions from an angel visitor, God has ways of letting us know his will. Think about the choices you will make today. Will they be a reflection of God's mercy? Pray earnestly that God will align your will and your choices with his own. Go back to God at the end of the day and listen.

> *Our Merciful Father in heaven,*
> *Hallowed be your name.*
> *Your kingdom come.*
> *Your will be done on earth as it is in heaven.*
>   *Amen.*

For insight concerning the original languages, I am indebted to William Barclay, *The Beatitudes and the Lord's Prayer for Everyman* (New York: Harper & Row, 1968), 60–65.

34
FOLLOWERS OF GOD

Be ye therefore *followers of God*, as dear children.

Ephesians 5:1 KJV

"Come, follow me," Jesus said. . . . At once they left their nets and followed him.

Matthew 4:19–20

The ancient Greeks invented a story that illustrates the dilemma sometimes faced by followers of God. When Orpheus, the human son of the Greek god Apollo, wed Eurydice, they delighted in making glorious music together and were very much in love. But the gods felt threatened by this. According to Greek mythology, these envious gods sent a poisonous snake to bite Eurydice, causing her death. Orpheus was inconsolable, weeping as he wandered the earth playing his lyre. The gods then decided to take pity on him, and invited him to journey through the underworld until he found his love. She could then follow him, retracing his long journey back to earth, where they could resume their married life. There were just two stipulations: Eurydice could not see Orpheus' face during their return journey, nor could she receive an explanation of what was happening.

To follow, at the outset and throughout, requires trust. Would Eurydice trust and follow her beloved even if she could not see his face and could not comprehend the circumstances? Was he really who he claimed to be? Following usually implies that the follower can't see or know everything the leader does.

To follow is to imitate. Most contemporary English translations of Ephesians 5:1 render the Greek "be imitators of God." Copy. Reproduce as accurately as possible. So we carefully follow Aunt Esther's recipe, hoping that the resulting lemon chiffon cake will be as delicious as hers. We painstakingly follow the diagrams in the instruction manual to the end that our new gas grill will look and function just like the one we saw in the store. We follow the route taken by the car ahead of us, hoping thus to arrive at our intended destination.

Following usually has an end in mind. Therefore, whom (or what) we follow makes an enormous difference—for trust is no virtue if it is misplaced. Followers seek a result; they want to reach a certain destination. Following begins with a single step. But for Eurydice and all would-be followers, it is more than that. It is an ongoing walk.

Jesus said, "I am the way and the truth and the life. No one comes to the Father except through me" (John 14:6). Jesus said, "I have prepared a place for you" (see John 14:2). Imitating Jesus is far from easy. We cannot always see his face. We don't always understand the path on which he takes us. The detours and ruts in the road frustrate us. Yet Jesus calls us to follow. People of God, we can trust *our* Bridegroom. Jesus will lead us home!

Claim the Name

Many people think they can assemble their bookcase or gas grill without reading the instruction manual. Are you one of them? God has given us an instruction manual. It is God's gift to us, especially at those times when we do not understand God's will and ways. Read it today, asking God to show you what your next step should be.

> *I am weak and I need your strength and power to endure with grace my weakest hour.*
> *Help me through the darkness your face to see. Lead me, O Lord, lead me.*
>
> *Lead me, guide me along the way, for if you lead me, I cannot stray.*
> *Lord, let me walk each day with you, lead me my whole life through.*
>
> *Help me walk in the paths of righteousness; be my aid when Satan and sin oppress.*

I am trusting you what e'er may be. Lead me, O Lord, lead me. Amen.

35

FISHERS OF MEN
AND WOMEN

As Jesus was walking beside the Sea of Galilee, he saw two brothers, Simon called Peter and his brother Andrew. They were casting a net into the lake, for they were fishermen. "Come, follow me," Jesus said, "and I will make you *fishers of men* [and *women*]."

Matthew 4:18–19

Galileans of Jesus' day ate little meat other than fish, with the result that fishing on the Sea of Galilee was big business. The names of the towns along the lake reflected this. Bethsaida means "fish town." Tarichaea, where fish were salted and packed for shipment, means "the place of salt fish." Each day fishermen in hundreds of small boats would cast their nets in the fruitful shallows just off shore. Preserving each night's catch in salt, washing and mending the two kinds of nets they used, repairing and maintaining the fishing boats, and negotiating with merchants kept Peter, Andrew, and their partners more than busy. And they were good at what they did.

But they had had an off night, one in which they had caught nothing. The next morning a rabbi came by and asked if he could stand in their boat just a bit off shore to make it easier for the crowd that had gathered to see and hear him. Now rabbis had certain areas of expertise, and Peter and Co. had theirs. But when the rabbi finished his teaching for the day, he offered these fishing experts fishing advice! "Row out past the shallows into the deep water, then let your nets down." Not the best time of day for fishing. Not ordinarily the best location for fish. Nonetheless, the fishermen did as the rabbi told them, and they caught so many fish their nets began to rip. They signaled for their partners to bring out a second boat. They filled both boats so full of fish they began to sink! This Jesus was no ordinary rabbi.

The fishermen found themselves unable to ignore or resist the invitation offered next by the rabbi Jesus. Ordinarily would-be disciples were the ones to ask if they might follow and learn from a rabbi. But this teacher was different in so many ways. "Follow me," he invited! "I'll teach you how to engage in an entirely new kind of fishing." So they pulled their boats up on shore, left everything, and followed him. Their vocation, their source of income, that with which they were familiar—they left it all behind.

But the qualities and strengths they had developed would be important in this new vocation. They were men well schooled in coping with every kind of weather. Even when they were cold and wet they had to be both patient and persistent. They had to be strong to haul in the heavy fish-filled nets. They knew they had something worth selling. They knew the fish they offered would satisfy and nourish. And they had learned how to persuade others to buy.

Patience, persistence, the ability to cope with adverse circumstances, strength, and the ability to sell were all valuable qualities when placed in the hand of the one who'd called them to be fishers of men and women. And what they would now offer was not simply nourishment for physical life but life eternal.

"Come follow me," Jesus invited a handful of Galilean fishermen. "Come follow me," Jesus invites you and me. "I will send you out to fish for people."

Claim the Name

Fishing goes along with following. If you claim to be a follower of Jesus, then fishing is part of your job description. Focus on what Jesus means to you, not on whether you think you're a good salesperson.

> *Rabbi Jesus,*
> *Show us how to fish today. Bless our efforts to draw others into your net. Amen.*

36

HEPHZIBAH

You will be called by a new name
    that the mouth of the LORD will bestow. . . .
No longer will they call you Deserted,
    or name your land Desolate.
But you will be called *Hephzibah* ["my delight is in
      her"],
    and your land Beulah;
for the LORD will take delight in you.

                              Isaiah 62:2, 4

Delight. Most of us have experienced it. If we've ever wondered why God created dandelions, it must surely be so that small children can, unadmonished, delightedly pick great bouquets of them to present to persons in whom they delight! We delight in what people do for us.

135

What mother or grandmother would not delight in the handmade card I received, laboriously inscribed, "hppy Muthr's day! 5 defrent things I like doing weth you," with the list following. But delighting in a person goes deeper than delighting in what that person does. It has everything to do with who the person is and the relationship we have with that person. To delight in someone is to enjoy that person and to find pleasure in simply being with him or her.

When you are delighted, do you jump up and down, maybe whoop a little? Or do those who know you well understand you are delighted when the corners of your lips curve upward, ever so slightly? Or do you express delight somewhere in the middle of those two extremes? How might the almighty God show delight? Isaiah says that God "will not keep silent . . . will not remain quiet, till her [Hephzibah's] righteousness shines out like the dawn, her salvation like a blazing torch" (62:1). The mouth of the Lord will give her a new name (62:2). Hephzibah's additional names include Holy People, the Redeemed of the Lord, Sought After (62:12).

But a reading of the book of Isaiah shows, time after time, the long-suffering Yahweh reaching out only to be spurned by the disobedient objects of his love. God's chosen have cut themselves off; they have been taken as exiles to live far from their now deserted and desolate homeland. The prophet acknowledges, "Our offenses are many in your sight, and our sins testify against us . . . rebellion and treachery against the LORD, turning our backs on our God, fomenting oppression and revolt, uttering lies our hearts have conceived. So justice is driven back, and righteousness stands at a distance; truth has stumbled in the streets, honesty cannot enter. Truth is nowhere to be found, and whoever shuns evil becomes a prey" (Isa. 59:12–15). Clearly the Lord's delight was not in what the people were being or doing.

So how do we make sense of this name Hephzibah, which means "my delight is in her"? Why is God delighted? The answer can be found in Isaiah 59:20, which reads, "The Redeemer will come to Zion, to those in Jacob who repent of their sins." This Redeemer has clothed the repentant people with garments of salvation and arrayed them in a robe of righteousness (Isa. 61:10). This new clothing represents a new, restored relationship. It is in that relationship that the Lord delights.

The face the Lord turns toward us is not one with clenched teeth and pursed lips. He does not dutifully put up with us because he is stuck with us. Clothed in the Redeemer's righteousness, we are called Hephzibah, for our God delights in us!

Claim the Name

The Lord delights in *you*! Thank him! The psalmist invites you to take delight in the Lord (Ps. 37:4). Try to do so today. When the Lord is truly your delight, you will find you are experiencing the desires of your heart.

> *O what wonder! How amazing!*
> *Jesus, glorious King of kings,*
> *Deigns to call me his beloved,*
> *Lets me rest beneath his wings. Amen.*
>
> Mary D. James, "All for Jesus," 1871

37

GOD'S TEMPLE

Don't you know that you yourselves are *God's temple*
and that God's Spirit lives in you? If anyone destroys
God's temple, God will destroy him; for *God's temple*
is sacred, and you are that temple.

1 Corinthians 3:16–17

All over the world throughout the centuries,
people have built temples. Some of them are
magnificent edifices that tourists flock to see.
Others are small and private. What temples have in
common is their builders' hope that the spirit of the
god or gods they worship will inhabit them.

The *Miyohoji O'Tera* is a Buddhist temple at the
end of the street where I lived as a child. It was only
a several minute walk from our Tokyo, Japan, home,
so I often watched as people entered the temple court-

yard by passing between two large stone lion-like creatures. The worshipers would begin by washing their hands and rinsing out their mouths, using the dipper provided. Then they would make their way to the temple itself. Before beginning to pray they would often clap their hands loudly or ring the brass gong hanging high above by pulling on its long rope. Would the washing of hands and mouth increase the chances that the worshipers would be considered worthy? Would the clapping and gong ringing increase the chances that the gods would hear and pay attention? These were the hopes of those who worshiped there.

Within Christendom the places where we worship together are almost never called temples. As the apostle Paul told the people of Athens (Acts 17:24), the God who made the world and everything in it, the Lord of heaven and earth whom we worship, does not live in temples built by human hands. Yahweh God has chosen instead to inhabit temples of his own creation—us!

We are God's temples. God's Spirit lives in us. No amount of hand or mouth cleansing could make us worthy, but God has done that for us in Jesus Christ. The Spirit of Yahweh God is attentive to our prayers around the clock every day of every week. There is no need for loud clapping or banging of a gong, for our God neither slumbers nor sleeps.

Yes, God has made us and God has made us worthy, but we are the temple caretakers. The way we eat, rest, and exercise affects the temple. What we read, listen to, and watch influences the temple. Our sexual activity impacts the temple. What kind of care is God's temple receiving from us? Do we honor the God we worship with our body (1 Cor. 6:20)?

If temple maintenance is a challenge for us, if we've been neglecting some aspects of it, there is help for us. We don't have to hope that God's Spirit will inhabit us; we can be certain of it! We have access to the power of the Holy Spirit, our temple resident, as we go about caring for the temple.

Claim the Name

What aspect of temple maintenance do you find most challenging? What first step might you take to improve your care of God's temple? Remember, you are not on your own. Pray for the Holy Spirit's help.

> *Creator Spirit, by whose aid the world's founda-*
> *tions first were laid,*
> *Come, visit every yearning mind; come, pour thy*
> *joys on humankind;*
> *From sin and sorrow set us free and make thy*
> *temples worthy thee. Amen.*
>
> John Dryden, "Creator Spirit, by Whose Aid," 1693

> *O Great Chief,*
> *Light a candle within my heart that I may see*
> *what is therein and sweep the rubbish from your*
> *dwelling place. Amen.*
>
> attributed to a young African girl, her name unknown,
> twentieth century

YOU SLUGGARD

Go to the ant, *you sluggard*;
    consider its ways and be wise!
It has no commander,
    no overseer or ruler,
yet it stores its provisions in summer
    and gathers its food at harvest.
How long will you lie there, *you sluggard*?
    When will you get up from your sleep?

Proverbs 6:6–10

The *sluggard* buries his hand in the dish;
    he is too lazy to bring it back to his mouth.
The *sluggard* is wiser in his own eyes
    than seven men who answer discreetly.

Proverbs 26:15–16

A sluggard is defined as habitually lazy, the ultimate in laziness. Not a name any of us likely wants to claim. And if sloth is not a sin that tempts you, you may feel free to skip this meditation!

So let's consider the ant: What is it about ants that the sluggard is urged to consider? Fifteen thousand species of ants inhabit all of the earth except the poles. These resourceful, industrious, self-directed insects live and work within colonies where there are clear divisions of labor. The queen lays the eggs, which are then fertilized by the male ants. The remaining work of the colony is highly specialized and divided among the female ants, those ants most likely to be observed by humans. These worker ants care for, protect, and feed one another. Nurse ants feed and clean larvae, carrying them to a different part of the nest if the room they are in becomes too wet or too cold. Other ants increase the size of the nest, adding passageways and more rooms as they are needed. They even clean out the rooms.

A colony of leaf-cutter ants can cut off all the leaves of a single tree in one night! With her sharp teeth, a leaf-cutter snips off a piece of leaf many times her own size, then carries it high above her back to the nest. Careful observation of a procession of leaf-cutters returning home may reveal a second smaller ant perched on top of the leaf. But these ants are not just along for the ride; they too have work to do. They are the "quality control" ants who make sure that no parasites are carried into the nest along with the leaf pieces. After the ants arrive back at the nest, they chew the leaf pieces into a damp mash, which they place in a special storage room. The spongy mushrooms that grow on these decomposing leaf pieces will be the food for this colony. Consider the ant, you sluggard!

A second folly of which the sluggard is warned is that of being wise in his own eyes. This loss of perspective may well be a result of slothfulness. The sluggard is too lazy even to feed himself (Prov. 26:15), let alone anyone else. There is no active involvement with the community, no looking to the needs of others, no working together. The sluggard simply fails to see the importance and value of others' contributions and perspectives. He doesn't see how much he needs others or others need him. The result is a highly inflated idea of the sluggard's own importance and wisdom.

People of God, there is much kingdom work to be done. This is no time for sluggards.

Claim the Name

What is the work God has called you to do? Are you doing it? Are there people to whom you go for wise counsel, who will speak the truth to you in love?

> *Prepare us, O God, "for works of service, so that the body of Christ may be built up until we all reach unity in the faith and in the knowledge of the Son of God and become mature, attaining to the whole measure of the fullness of Christ. Then we will no longer be infants, tossed back and forth by the waves, and blown here and there by every wind of teaching and by the cunning and craftiness of [deceitful schemers]. Instead, speaking the truth in love, we will in all things grow up into him who is the Head, that is,*

143

Christ. From him the whole body, joined and held together by every supporting ligament, grows and builds itself up in love, as each part does its work." Amen.

Ephesians 4:12–16

39
CHRISTIANS

For a whole year Barnabas and Saul met with the church and taught great numbers of people. The disciples were called *Christians* first at Antioch.

Acts 11:26

However, if you suffer as a *Christian*, do not be ashamed, but praise God that you bear that name.

1 Peter 4:16

"Christian" is used by some as a catchall for theists who are not Buddhists, Jews, or followers of Islam. It is really a name derived from "Christ," which is another way of saying "Messiah," or "Savior." Many Jews of Jesus' day expected the Messiah to come in a blaze of power, perhaps leading massive armies who would crush their oppressor,

Rome. Jesus, the Christ, was not the Messiah they were expecting. Jesus, the Christ, was headed not to Rome but to die on a cross mounted on a garbage heap outside Jerusalem.

Christians then are followers of Jesus Christ, people of the cross. Many within Christendom are accustomed to seeing crucifixes in their places of worship—crosses that depict the suffering and death of Jesus. But when the musical *Jesus Christ, Superstar* made its debut in the early 1970s, some Christians objected, particularly to its ending. The musical colorfully portrayed King Herod's raucous taunting of Jesus in a manner faithful to Scripture. Pontius Pilate was likewise depicted faithfully, as a man both powerful and insecure. It was the ending that some objected to. The actor portrayed Jesus on the cross, dead, as the curtains closed. The musical ended giving no hint of the resurrection of Jesus that would take place three days later.

Some years after the musical originally opened, a lighting designer in Detroit's Fox Theater got it right. The musical came to the end as scripted, with the actor playing the role of Jesus hanging on the cross. The theater was made completely dark. In the darkness the actor was released from the cross and left the stage. Then lights placed all around the border of the cross were turned on. The performance ended with the empty cross framed in blazing light!

As Barnabas and Saul taught the Antiochians, God demonstrates love for us in many ways, but they all point to the love shown by Jesus' death on the cross. We are people of the cross because the cross freed us from a death that should have been ours. We would otherwise have been the ones separated from God, and that separation would have lasted eternally.

Less than 1 percent of Japan's population professes to be Christian. A leader from a thriving Buddhist sect once advised a Christian missionary, "You Christians would be so much more successful if you'd give up that bloody atonement story." The cross didn't and doesn't market well. It was, after all, the most common means of executing criminals used in the first century. As a measurement of success, death on the cross was about as low as one could go. The apostle Paul wrote, "The message of the cross is foolishness to those who are perishing, but to us who are being saved it is the power of God" (1 Cor. 1:18). By claiming the name Christian, we identify ourselves with Jesus Christ, the one who died on the cross for us.

For some followers of the cross, claiming to be a Christian has meant more than being taunted or being considered naive or intellectually inferior. For some it has meant untimely, often cruel, physical death. Stephen, Peter, Paul, Thomas, and others of Jesus' first followers led the procession of those martyred in Jesus' name. Peter reminds us all, "If you suffer as a Christian, do not be ashamed, but praise God that you bear that name" (1 Peter 4:16).

What if the story ended with Jesus' body on the cross? What if Jesus' death and the deaths of all who have died claiming his name have been a noble but futile effort? We have a multitude of faithful witnesses, some of whom have staked their lives on it, who proclaim otherwise. The lighting designer was right. Light has pierced the darkness, revealing the unoccupied cross and the empty tomb. Christ died for us on the cross. Christ is risen. Christ will come again!

Claim the Name

"Jesus said to her [Martha], 'I am the resurrection and the life. Anyone who believes in me will live, even though they die; and whoever lives by believing in me will never die. Do you believe this?'" (John 11:25–26 TNIV). Can you answer as Martha did (John 11:27)?

> *Lord Jesus Christ,*
> *When I survey the wondrous cross, on which the*
>   *Prince of glory died,*
> *My richest gain I count but loss, and pour contempt*
>   *on all my pride.*
>
> *Forbid it, Lord, that I should boast, save in the*
>   *death of Christ, my God!*
> *All the vain things that charm me most, I sacrifice*
>   *them through his blood.*
>
> *Were the whole realm of nature mine, that were*
>   *a present far too small.*
> *Love so amazing, so divine, demands my soul, my*
>   *life, my all. Amen.*
>
> Isaac Watts, "When I Survey the Wondrous Cross," 1707

40

BEZALEEL

The Lord said to Moses: Take notice! I have called by name *Bezaleel*, the son of Uri, the son of Hur, of the tribe of Judah and have filled him with God's Spirit in skill, intelligence and understanding for all craftsmanship to plan designs in gold, silver and bronze work, for cutting precious stones for setting, for woodcarving and for all sorts of craftwork . . . to make everything I have ordered you—the meeting tent, . . . the table and its utensils, the pure lampstand . . . the altar of incense, the altar of burnt offering . . . the washbasin . . . the sacred garments for Aaron the priest . . . the anointing oil and the perfumed incense for the sanctuary—have them work it out just as I have ordered you.

Exodus 31:1–11 MLB

Take notice! The Lord here calls into his service an artist—and not to leave behind his art and teach Sunday school! The name Bezaleel means "in the shadow and protection of God." What do we know about this man?

Bezaleel was of the tribe of Judah, son of Uri, and grandson of Hur. This could have been the Hur who helped hold up Moses' hands as Moses prayed during the battle of Rephidim (Exod. 17:12). Bezaleel was filled with God's Spirit. He was obedient to God (Exod. 38:22). He himself was highly skilled in a variety of arts and could instruct and oversee others (Exod. 35:30–34). He was creative and able to make artistic designs (Exod. 35:31–33). He was a good steward of the people's offerings, even letting them know when he had received enough (Exod. 36:4–5). He could follow the Lord's instructions (Exod. 36:1).

Bezaleel was called on to make the place for worship that would travel with the Israelites during their years in the wilderness. He and the artisans who worked under him created the Tent of Meeting and all its furnishings, as well as the formal clothing the priests would wear. The ark itself was made of acacia wood and covered inside and out with pure gold. It contained the tablets on which the Ten Commandments were carved, a jar of the manna that fed the Israelites in the wilderness, and Aaron's rod, which had budded. Over the top of the ark was the mercy seat, or atonement cover. It was made of pure gold, and a sculpted cherub was a part of each end. It must have been exquisite! Bezaleel attached two gold rings to each side of the ark and placed gold poles through them. When the Israelites relocated, the priests carried the ark using these poles, for after Bezaleel had completed his work, no human was ever to touch the ark and live! He himself must have been under the protection of God as he worked.

This Spirit-inspired creation of Bezaleel's occupied a special part of the Holy Place inside the Tent of Meeting—it was the place where the Spirit of the holy God chose to be. This Most Holy Place was entered only by the high priest, only once a year on the Day of Atonement. There the high priest offered a sacrifice on his own behalf as well as for the sins of the people.

It is important to note that Israel's place of worship was made beautiful at God's initiative. In the truest sense of the word, ours is indeed a beautiful God, one who wants to be worshiped beautifully.

Claim the Name

What have I been given with which I could worship God beautifully? Who do I know whom I could encourage to use their artistic gifts in the praise and worship of God?

> *Beautiful Savior! King of Creation!*
> *Son of God and Son of Man!*
> *Truly I'd love thee, truly I'd serve thee,*
> *Light of my soul, my joy, my crown.*
>
> *Beautiful Savior! Lord of the nations!*
> *Son of God and Son of Man!*
> *Glory and honor, praise, adoration,*
> *Now and forever more be thine. Amen.*

"Fairest Lord Jesus," 1873

FAITHFUL

Paul, an apostle of Christ Jesus by the will of God, to
. . . the *faithful* in Christ Jesus.

Ephesians 1:1

Now faith is being sure of what we hope for and certain
of what we do not see. . . . Abel . . . Enoch . . . Noah . . .
Abraham . . . Isaac . . . Jacob . . . Joseph . . . [Jochebed
and Amram] . . . Moses . . . Rahab . . . Gideon . . . Barak
. . . Samson . . . Jephthah . . . David . . . Samuel . . . the
prophets . . . these were all commended for their faith,
yet none of them received what had been promised.
God had planned something better for us so that only
together with us would they be made perfect.

from Hebrews 11

Faithful. It may feel presumptuous for us to claim
many of the names given to the people of God,
and this one in particular. Faithful? How full?
What if our faith is no bigger than the tiny speck of

a mustard seed (Matt. 17:20)? Consider Rahab the prostitute, whose story we read in Joshua 2. Her life prior to this point had not been particularly faithful. And what if there are times when we who are called faithful fail to demonstrate any faith at all? Consider Abraham's story in Genesis 12:10–13. Out of fear he told Sarai to pretend she was his sister. What if, acting on our own impulses, we have done something truly unbecoming a faithful one, something really wrong? Consider the story of Jephthah the judge found in Judges 11:30–40 and that of David found in 2 Samuel 11. Yet Rahab, Abraham, Jephthah, and David "were all commended for their faith" (Heb. 11:39).

Consider the faith of Jochebed, mother of Moses, faithful daughter of God. Do you suppose she had hoped for another daughter? A daughter would have been spared (Exod. 1:22). But God gave her a baby boy, a son she nursed but did not name (Exod. 2:7–10). Being sure of what she hoped for, she used her God-given creativity to make for him a strong water-tight basket and placed her precious baby in the river Nile—certain of what she could not see.

Fast-forward to Moses' young adulthood. Jochebed's son is wanted for murder, and the authorities are after him (Exod. 2:11–15). Jochebed's miracle baby is fleeing for his life. We can imagine her heavy heart. Surely God must have spared her son for something more than this! But Jochebed had the stuff of things hoped for, the evidence of things not seen.

We don't know if Jochebed lived to see the amazing events of Exodus 14:21–31, or if she sang along with her children Moses and Miriam (Exodus 15) as they praised God for their deliverance from Egypt. But years earlier she had claimed with certainty the evidence of things she had not yet seen on behalf of her children.

Jochebed's faithfulness was not something she developed on her own or exhibited in her own strength. Nor can we claim the name faithful as our own accomplishment. It is only in Christ Jesus that we can be sure of what we do not see. It is only in Christ Jesus that we dare add our names to the list of faithful given in Hebrews 11.

Being faithful is not really about us at all. As with all the names we share with Jesus, we only dare claim it because of him (Rev. 1:5). With Jochebed and the others, we are among the faithful in Christ Jesus!

Claim the Name

A faithful one is reliable, a keeper of promises, so the word of a faithful one is as good as the promised action.

To be faithful is to base the certainty of what we hope for but cannot see on what we have seen and on *whom* we do know.

To be faithful is to wrap ourselves in the faithfulness of the only one who is *truly* faithful!

Today you are invited to add your name to the Hebrews 11 listing of faithful Old Testament people.

> *Our heavenly Father,*
>   *Today we thank you that we can take comfort in the confidence that we belong, body and soul, in life and in death, to our faithful Savior Jesus Christ. Amen.*

from the Heidelberg Catechism's reponse to question #1

42
OUTSIDERS

After this he [Jesus] went out and saw a man named Levi at his work collecting taxes. Jesus said, "Come along with me." And he did—walked away from everything and went home with him.

Levi gave a large dinner at his home for Jesus. Everybody was there, tax men and other disreputable characters as guests at the dinner. The Pharisees and their religion scholars came to his disciples greatly offended. "What is he doing eating and drinking with crooks and 'sinners'?"

Jesus heard about it and spoke up, "Who needs a doctor: the healthy or the sick? I'm here inviting *outsiders*, not insiders—an invitation to a changed life, changed inside and out."

Luke 5:27–32 Message

T ax collectors were not particularly loved by anybody. They were always locals, but they acted under the aegis of the Roman Empire.

Rome turned a blind eye to the fact that most collectors demanded more than the required revenue so as to skim off the extra for themselves. But there was job security, and it provided a more than adequate income. Their practices had made them outsiders. They were not Romans, only employees of their captors. That, and the fact that they could get away with their cheating, caused them to be despised and considered outsiders by their Jewish neighbors.

Jesus had the audacity to invite Levi (or Matthew) the tax collector to leave behind his job security and his wealth and to follow him. And Levi did exactly that.

Levi launched his new life by throwing a big retirement party. But instead of taking the seat of honor for himself, he gave that position to Jesus, his new employer. The guests at the party were other tax collectors and outsiders like Levi himself. The proper people, the religious insiders, were now standing outside in the courtyard, where the fragrant aroma of the delicious feast did nothing to quash the rumbling of their empty stomachs or the rumbling of their complaints.

"The nerve of your 'holy' rabbi!" they call out to Jesus' disciples. "Partying with outsiders! What does he think he's doing, accepting an invitation like this one?"

Jesus himself responds. It is he who has extended an invitation. His invitation is addressed to outsiders, not insiders. It is an invitation to a changed life. Jesus' response invites his hearers to rethink the question: Who is the insider and who is the outsider in this story? And Jesus' response prompts us to ask: Who are the twenty-first-century Levis? Whether we have always seen ourself as an outsider or have never seen ourself as an outsider is inconsequential, for we are all outsiders until Jesus comes to include us. Regardless of our educational level or skin color, our physical or mental capacity, our sexual orientation, or our style of worship, we are all outsiders. Without regard to our income level, whether we have AIDS, a prison record, or have had an abortion, we, along with Levi, are the ones Jesus calls.

Excluding others—pushing someone else outside— is often a characteristic of would-be insiders. But Jesus did not come to exclude. His invitation is for those outsiders standing hungry in the courtyard as well as for those already feasting at the table. "I'm here inviting outsiders, not insiders," Jesus says. It's "an invitation to a changed life, changed inside and out." And you, whoever you are and whatever your past has been, are included with Levi the tax collector as the intended recipient of Jesus' gracious invitation.

Claim the Name

The name *outsider* is a paradox. Only by claiming this name can we be truly included! Today celebrate the fact that you are named outsider. It is for you that Jesus came. Be on the lookout for other outsiders to whom you might extend Jesus' gracious invitation.

Jesus, our radical Lord and Master,
Thank you for inviting us outsiders to your
table. Forgive us for all the energy we waste trying

to force our way in and trying to push others out. Humbled at what it has cost you to include us, we accept your gracious invitation with grateful hearts. Our desire is to follow you. Open our eyes to see others around us with whom we may share this invitation. Amen.

43

GOD'S CO-WORKERS

For we are God's *co-workers*.
1 Corinthians 3:9 TNIV

It was the custom of Janet Lutz, a hospital chaplain in Atlanta, Georgia, to go about the hospital where she served and offer to pray for the hands of those who worked there. Often she would pray for those doing the more menial tasks, such as cleaning the bathrooms, washing trays, and serving food in the cafeteria. In a windowless basement room of the hospital, she discovered a woman whose job was to select and package the instruments needed for each surgery. She would receive a list that included the patient's name, the type of surgery, and each tool or item needed to perform it. Her job required precision and careful attention to details—for an error could have costly consequences. As Chaplain Lutz talked with her, she discovered that as this woman collected and packaged the instruments, she prayed by name for the patient who would be having the surgery, a person she did not know and would likely never meet. This had been her practice for forty years!

This prayerful packer of surgical instruments was one of God's co-workers. God has a multitude of co-workers, and their tasks include many things we may never have considered or even imagined. (The apostle Paul could not have imagined the work this woman did!)

Do we think our work is too mundane, too "un-spiritual" for us to be considered God's co-worker? A hospital chaplain would surely qualify, but someone who packs surgical instruments? If I am where God wants me to be, doing work God has placed in front of me, then it is God's work. God's idea of what is more important and less important work may have no correlation to how we humans view it.

Perhaps we have been doing God's work and are feeling burned out, worn out, and alone. The prophet Elijah had that experience (1 Kings 18–19). He had just prayed for and witnessed several mighty miracles. After the prophets of Baal had retreated in utter fail-ure, Elijah's Yahweh had poured out fire from heaven, which had completely consumed the water-drenched bull that had been placed on the altar as a sacrifice to the Lord. Elijah prayed, and God sent rain to the land that had been parched with drought.

After all this, one might guess that Elijah would have reached a spiritual high. Instead, he cowered, fled, and hid when the wicked Queen Jezebel, seemingly undaunted, threatened. Elijah whimpered to God, "I am the only one left, and now they are trying to kill me too." Yahweh in his mercy came to this faithful co-worker and assured him that seven thousand more of God's co-workers could be found in Israel. Elijah was not alone!

Like Elijah and the packer of surgical instruments, God's co-workers are people of prayer. Like Elijah, they sometimes feel abandoned and discouraged. But God's co-workers are never alone. They span the centuries and they circle the globe!

Claim the Name

Prayerfully make your work for this day an offering to God. Pray for eyes to see that, as God's co-worker, you are not alone.

> The sure provisions of my God attend me all my days;
> O may your house be my abode, and all my work be praise.
> There would I find a settled rest, while others go and come;
> No more a stranger, or a guest, but like a child at home. Amen.

Isaac Watts, "My Shepherd Will Supply My Need," 1719

The story about Janet Lutz was taken from one of National Public Radio's StoryCorps offerings, aired December 19, 2008.

44

ABRAHAM

When Abram was ninety-nine years old, the LORD appeared to him and said, "I am God Almighty [*Elohim Shaddai*]; walk before me and be blameless. I will confirm my covenant between me and you and will greatly increase your numbers."

Abram fell facedown, and God said to him, "As for me, this is my covenant with you: . . . No longer will you be called Abram; your name will be *Abraham*, for I have made you a father of many nations."

Genesis 17:1–5

By faith *Abraham*, when called to go . . . obeyed and went.

Hebrews 11:8

By faith *Abraham*, even though he was past age . . . was enabled to become a father because he considered him faithful who had made the promise.

Hebrews 11:11

By faith *Abraham*, when God tested him, offered Isaac
as a sacrifice.

Hebrews 11:17

The New Testament presents Abraham as an
outstanding example of those who believe,
who live by a faith in God expressed in obedience. It is also true that Abraham was a flawed and
sinful human being. Twice when fearing for his own
life he lied and said that his beautiful wife, Sarai, was
his sister, thus allowing her to be taken temporarily as
the wife of another. Yet Scripture commends him for
his faithfulness, and he was called a friend of God.

Abraham obeyed and trusted God, even when it
meant leaving all that was familiar, pulling up all his
roots. As he prepared to leave his home in the city
of Ur, he couldn't check out his "new digs" on the
internet. At the outset he didn't even know where
God was leading him. His faith meant confidence in
the one he was following.

Abraham obeyed and trusted God, even when what
God was telling him was physically impossible. Sarai
was ninety years old—long past menopause. How
could she conceive and carry a child? How could
Abraham father many nations? His faith meant
confidence in the one who could do the humanly
impossible.

Abraham obeyed and trusted God, even when he
thought it would mean losing the son he loved more
than anything or anyone in the world. His faith meant
confidence in the one who could make right the greatest wrong he could have imagined.

Faith, according to the writer of Hebrews, considers things hoped for as though they were concrete and tangible. Faith in our God *Elohim* (almighty) *Shaddai* (nourishing and nurturing) means that even something we can't see is as good as done. *Elohim Shaddai* is the God who can make ninety-nine-year-old Abraham a father. *Elohim Shaddai* is the God who can be trusted to lead Abraham and all his family to a good place. *Elohim Shaddai* is the God who can spare Isaac when the knife that would kill him is in mid-stroke.

There are important and encouraging things for us to note about the faith of Abraham. First, *in whom* that faith is placed is of vital importance. Often today we hear people use the word *faith* without a stated or even implied object, as though that didn't matter. It does matter! Second, even a person of great faith, such as Abraham, had seasons of doubt—times when he just plain blew it. Jesus is the only one who is all the time, throughout all time and eternity, faithful. It is Jesus' faithfulness, credited to Abraham, that God honors (Gal. 3:6). And it is Jesus' faithfulness, credited to us, that God honors (Gal. 3:7–9).

Claim the Name

We never can prove the delights of his love until
    all on the altar we lay;
For the favor he shows and the joy he bestows are
    for those who will trust and obey.

Then in fellowship sweet we will sit at his feet,
    or we'll walk by his side in the way;

What he says we will do, where he sends we will
go—never fear only trust and obey.

Trust and obey, for there's no other way to be
happy in Jesus but to trust and obey.

John H. Sammis, "Trust and Obey," 1887

*The God of Abraham praise, who reigns enthroned
above,*
The ancient of eternal days, the God of love!
*The Lord, the great I AM, by earth and heaven
confessed—*
*We bow before his holy name forever blest.
Amen.*

Thomas Olivers, "The God of Abraham Praise," 1765

45

LIVING STONES

And you are *living stones* that God is building into his spiritual temple.

1 Peter 2:5 NLT

Stones. Anyone playing "Twenty Questions" would give as the first clue the category "mineral," the only one of the three categories—animal, vegetable, mineral—designated for things that are not and never have been alive. But living stones? It's an oxymoron. A contradiction in terms.

Stones of different sizes and sorts are put to many uses. Scripture elsewhere speaks of a stone used as a pillow. Stones were used as altars, reminders, and on one occasion to fell a giant. But in this text, living stones are used by God as something with which to build.

Stones are a better choice of building material than most other options. They won't be consumed by fire. They will neither rot nor rust. They won't break easily. They are more likely to prevail against strong winds or storms. Their inherent insulating capacity protects against both heat and cold. But despite all this, stones don't breathe or move without help, nor do they grow as living plants and creatures do. For ordinary stones to become living stones has everything to do with the builder. From the beginning when the earth's foundations were laid, the builder, God, has had a plan. The placement of each stone in relation to the others is part of that plan.

Living stones would be an impossibility were it not for Jesus Christ, the original Living Stone. Some have not recognized Jesus for who he is and have rejected him. Some, in their hurry to pursue their own ambitions, have tripped over the Living Stone.

But Jesus is the source from whom we derive our life. The Spirit of Jesus transforms us from lifeless minerals into living stones. Jesus is the capstone of the arch, holding all the other living stones in place. Jesus is the cornerstone of the foundation, against which all the other stones are aligned.

And notice what is being built. A temple! As noted in meditation 37, builders erect temples with the idea that their god will live in them. Our God is both the temple builder and the temple resident. It is within us living stones that the Holy Spirit of the living God has chosen to live. And it is the Holy Spirit who makes us alive.

Claim the Name

Has the Spirit breathed life into you, or are you still simply stone, mineral? Have all your efforts to breathe life into yourself, by yourself, exhausted you? Have you run blindly into the Living Stone, stumbled, and fallen? Jesus longs to help you up, to breathe his life into you. Will you take his extended hand?

In Christ alone my hope is found;
He is my light, my strength, my song;
This cornerstone, this solid ground,
Firm through the fiercest drought and storm.
What heights of love, what depths of peace,
When fears are stilled, when strivings cease!
My comforter, my all in all,
Here in the love of Christ I stand.

No guilt in life, no fear in death,
This is the pow'r of Christ in me;
From life's first cry to final breath,
Jesus commands my destiny.
No pow'r of hell, no scheme of man,
Can ever pluck me from his hand;
Till he returns or calls me home,
Here in the pow'r of Christ I'll stand. Amen.

46

THE GREATEST

An argument started among the disciples as to which of them would be *the greatest*. Jesus, knowing their thoughts, took a little child and had him stand beside him. Then he said to them, "Whoever welcomes this little child in my name welcomes me; and whoever welcomes me welcomes the one who sent me. For whoever is least among you all is *the greatest*."

Luke 9:46–48 TNIV

His older cousin was all too quick to remind him of that fact. At last his third birthday arrived. "Now I'm three too!" he proudly announced. Without missing a beat she replied, "But I'm three-er."

Who is the greatest? Humans have argued variations of that question for almost as long as there have been humans, and Jesus' disciples were no exception. Accomplishments, stature and physical prowess, accumulation of wealth, popularity, and prestige are some of the things we use to measure greatness. But God turns our human measuring sticks upside down. The first are last. The last are first. Unlike us, God assesses greatness from the inside out.

The prophet Samuel learned that lesson. He was sent by the Lord to the home of Jesse to anoint one of Jesse's sons as the next king of Israel (1 Samuel 16). Jesse's eldest, Eliab, was an impressive-looking young man, and Samuel thought he was surely to be the next king. But the Lord cautioned Samuel not to consider his appearance or his height. God had rejected Eliab. Humans may look at the outward appearance, but the Lord looks at the heart.

What is the yardstick the Lord uses for measuring greatness? Not the eldest, the handsomest, the tallest, the richest, the smartest, or the most talented. "The greatest among you," Jesus said, "is the one who welcomes and shows hospitality to someone small and vulnerable, such as this child. The greatest among you will be your servant" (see Luke 9:47–48).

The best servants rarely call attention to themselves. The best servants are intent on making the master and the ones served look good. Their hard work and attention to detail may go unnoticed because everything goes smoothly.

True greatness is neither sought nor grasped. True greatness is never achieved by pushing another down or out of the way. True greatness is being like Jesus.

Claim the Name

"Do nothing out of selfish ambition or vain conceit, but in humility consider others better than yourselves. Each of you should look not only to your own interests, but also to the interests of others. Your attitude should be the same as Christ Jesus: Who, being in the very nature God, did not consider equality with God something to be grasped, but made himself nothing, taking the very nature of a servant" (Phil. 2:3–7).

Great and gracious God,

In the person of Jesus you have shown us true greatness.

In the person of Jesus you have modeled servanthood.

May we this day seek to be like him. Amen.

47

THE CHURCH

[Jesus] is the head of the body, *the church*; he is the beginning and the firstborn from among the dead, so that in everything he might have the supremacy.

Colossians 1:18

On this rock I [Jesus] will build my *church*, and the gates of Hades will not overcome it.

Matthew 16:18

Five thousand pieces!" proclaimed the cover of the puzzle box. The bright yellow letters were splashed across the photo depicting what the completed puzzle would look like. Aunt Irene had purchased the puzzle at a garage sale for twenty-five cents and had brought it with her to the family reunion. Over the course of the week many family members worked on it. Some spent an occasional few minutes sorting similarly colored pieces into piles or locating two or three pieces that fit together. Others pored over the puzzle for hours at a time. At last 4,999 pieces had been put into place, but the box was empty. One small empty space remained! One missing piece stood in the way of the puzzle's completion.

In the church of Jesus every piece matters. It is incomplete otherwise. Scripture offers us the metaphor of the human body to help us understand the church. Anyone who has ever accidentally smashed the tip of her thumb knows how the pain of one small body part impacts the entire body. Each part matters! Some body parts are more visible and perhaps appear to be more important, but never underestimate the value of the small, unseen organs. Ask anyone who's ever had a thyroid gland malfunction.

What comes to your mind when you hear the words "the church"? A particular denomination or branch of Christendom? Perhaps you have a mental picture of your own place of worship or a place where you once worshiped. Perhaps you think of the people who make up your church family. They are truly your blood relatives—related to you because of the shed blood of Jesus.

The church was born during the first Feast of Pentecost that followed Jesus' ascension into heaven. Jesus' followers had gathered in an upper room, no doubt out of obedience to his instructions but perhaps also simply because they needed to be together, as family members often do following the loss of a loved one.

They ate, they talked, they wept, they prayed. Suddenly a sound like the blowing of a violent wind came from heaven and filled the house where they were sitting. Flames of fire appeared to separate, and a little flame came to rest on each of them. The body of Jesus received the promised Spirit of Jesus that day! The church of Jesus spans the globe and all the centuries between that day of Pentecost and our own.

Perhaps when you think of the church you are grateful. Through her your faith has grown, you have been well cared for and nurtured, and with her you have found meaningful ways to serve. Thanks be to God!

Perhaps when you think of the church you are frustrated, or bitter, or angry. You have been hurt by some members of the church. Your attempts to serve have been squelched or misunderstood. You have felt neither cared for nor nurtured. God seems distant. Your puzzle piece has been missing from the box, and no one seems to know or care.

The church is made up of sinners still being made holy. When we pay too much attention to these not-yet-holy folk (including ourselves), it is easy to sink into frustration, bitterness, or anger. The only remedy is the one given to Peter as he attempted to walk on the waves of the Sea of Galilee. The only thing that prevented Peter from sinking was looking at Jesus. Walking on water is a miracle—humanly speaking it can't be done. Being the church is also a miracle—humanly speaking it can't be done. It is only possible if we keep our eyes on Jesus, our head.

Jesus is building his church. It will be incomplete unless your piece is part of the picture.

Claim the Name

I am the church! You are the church! We are the
church together!
All who follow Jesus, all around the world, yes,
we're the church together!

The church is not a building, the church is not
a steeple,
The church is not a resting place; the church is
a people!

We're many kinds of people with many kinds
of faces,
All colors and all ages too, from all times and
places.

At Pentecost some people received the Holy
Spirit
And told the good news through the world to
all who would hear it.

*Now to him who is able to do immeasurably
more than all we ask or imagine, according to
his power that is at work within us, to him be glory
in the church and in Christ Jesus throughout all
generations, for ever and ever! Amen.*

Ephesians 3:20–21

48
LAZARUS

Jesus called in a loud voice, "*Lazarus*, come out!" The dead man came out, his hands and feet wrapped with strips of linen and a cloth around his face. Jesus said to them, "Take off the grave clothes and let him go."

John 11:43–44

"Lazarus, come out!" Now there was a dramatic wake-up call! Lazarus had been dead for four days, and his sister Martha was concerned about the odor she expected if his tomb were opened. But she obeyed Jesus and had the stone removed from the entrance to the tomb. Then the once dead Lazarus responded to Jesus' summons.

One wonders if Lazarus saw the additional time for him to spend on earth as a reprieve or as an extended sentence. Lazarus and his sisters were dear friends of

Jesus, and he, along with Martha, surely trusted Jesus for his eternal life (John 11:24–27). Could Lazarus recall anything from the four days his body lay dead in the tomb? What might he have been thinking as he blinked his eyes in the sunlight once again and saw the incredulous faces of his sisters and friends?

Jesus leaves us with no uncertainty about the main reason he did this miracle and why it has been recorded for us. It was so that the observers that day, as well as those who would later read about it, might believe (John 11:42; 20:31). The miracle was done to bring God glory (John 11:40).

We don't know anything about what Lazarus thought as he walked out of his tomb, his burial wrapping still dragging. And we don't know anything about what Lazarus did with his additional earthly life. But we share more with Lazarus than we may at first realize.

The apostle Paul makes it very clear that the outcome of our sin is certain death. We died, says Paul, and we have, by our baptism, been buried with Christ. Like Lazarus, we have emerged to live a new life in Christ (Romans 6).

Lazarus' resurrection offers us, as well as any of Jesus' first-century followers who might later have reflected on it, a bridge between the Friday and the Sunday of Holy Week. Although Friday may be where we are living now, Tony Campolo reminds us in his now famous sermon, ". . . Sunday's coming!" But we twenty-first-century followers of Jesus have been given significantly more than those first followers who grieved his death. Sunday *has* come! Jesus *is* risen! We live *between* two Sundays.

Lazarus was given an extra inning for his earthly life. But so were we. Even though we don't know what Lazarus did with his extra gift of time, we can determine what we will do with ours. Being near physical death, then being spared, has often filled people with gratitude and a new perspective. Should that not be even more true of us? Paul urges us, "Offer yourselves to God, as those who have been brought from death to life; and offer the parts of your body to him as instruments of righteousness" (Rom. 6:13).

Do we even think of our hands or our ears as being "instruments of righteousness" to be used for God's glory? What might one do with an instrument of righteousness? Are there things we should not do with such an instrument? The first question and answer of the Westminster Catechism suggest that the chief goal for Lazarus and his kin ought to be "to glorify God and to enjoy him forever." Take off your grave clothes and go!

Claim the Name

If this were an extra day on earth given you after your own funeral service, how would you use it? What specific things would you do?

> Lord Jesus,
> [You speak], and listening to [your] voice, new
>   life the dead receive;
> The mournful, broken hearts rejoice; the humble
>   poor believe.

*To God all glory, praise and love be now and
ever given
By saints below and saints above; the church in
earth and heaven. Amen.*

Charles Wesley, "O for a Thousand Tongues to Sing," 1739

49

PEACEMAKERS

Blessed are the *peacemakers*,
  for they will be called children of God.

Matthew 5:9 TNIV

Peacemakers who sow in peace raise a harvest of righteousness.

James 3:18

On the evening of that first day of the week, when the disciples were together, with the doors locked for fear of the Jews, Jesus came and stood among them and said, "Peace be with you!" After he said this, he showed them his hands and side. The disciples were overjoyed when they saw the Lord. Again Jesus said, "Peace be with you! As the Father has sent me, I am sending you."

John 20:19–21

But now in Christ Jesus you who once were far away have been brought near through the blood of Christ. For he himself is our peace.

Ephesians 2:13–14

The whip he'd made himself whistled through the air of the temple courtyard. Tables were turned on end, coins were scattered all over the paving stones—no one knew who owned what! Doves, which would have been sacrifices, were flying freely. The sheep and cattle would-be sacrifices were also given at least a temporary reprieve. Yelling. Mooing. Bleating. Cooing. The truest peacemaker of all time was at work!

Many of us who live in the twenty-first century have an anemic, incomplete understanding of the word *peace*. Often what we mean is "without war" or "without conflict or disturbance." But peace is more than tranquility. Peacemaking is more than simply peace-wanting, peace-loving, or even peace-living. Avoiding confrontation is not peacemaking. Sweeping the dirt under the rug is not peacemaking. Being a peacemaker often means getting down on our knees and scrubbing away at the stench and the mud.

When Jesus speaks of peace, he means a full-orbed wholeness. This is the meaning behind the greeting "shalom," or "salaam," still used today by our Middle Eastern friends. Imagine yourself, having been made one with God, standing at the center of a sphere. This sphere contains all the people and all the things— both human-made and natural—that touch your life in any way. You have a just and right relationship with every person in the sphere, and each of them is rightly related to each other and to God. No one needs or wants anything. Everyone and everything is healthy and whole.

This picture of peace will not come about in its entirety until Jesus comes again. But this is the peace Jesus is talking about. It is toward this end that peacemakers are to be working now. And this picture of peace could never happen were it not for the horrific, violent death of Jesus on the cross, in order that our relationship with God could be made whole. His peacemaking makes possible our small attempts at it. Jesus is truly our peace.

If the New Testament writers had known about DNA, perhaps the text would have read, "Blessed are the peacemakers, in this they exhibit the DNA of God!" The Hebrew language has few adjectives, so to describe a person, to get at the essence of who he was, the phrase "son of . . ." was often used. Barnabas was known as the "son of encouragement," and James and John were the "sons of thunder." We, as we seek to be peacemakers, will be called "sons (and daughters) of God," for peacemakers are made of the very stuff of God!

Bless you in your peacemaking. "May the peace of God, which transcends all understanding, . . . guard your hearts and your minds in Christ Jesus" (Phil. 4:7).

 *Claim the Name*

If you have never received Christ's peace, that is the place to start.

Read Matthew 5:1–12 (often known as the Beatitudes). These are the characteristics of *kingdom citizens*. Unlike spiritual gifts, or talents, a kingdom citizen is meant to display all these characteristics, each in concert with the others. Being a peacemaker is only possible as we see ourselves to be truly poor in spirit, as we mourn all that is not the way it's supposed to be, as we are meek, as we hunger and thirst for righteousness, as we are merciful, as we are pure in heart, and as we are persecuted for righteousness.

Lord, make me an instrument of your peace.
Where there is hatred, let me sow love,
Where there is injury, pardon,
Where there is doubt, faith,
Where there is despair, hope,
Where there is darkness, light,
Where there is sadness, joy.

O Divine Master, grant that I may not so much seek
to be consoled as to console,
to be understood as to understand,
to be loved as to love.
For it is in giving that we receive.
It is in pardoning that we are pardoned,
It is in dying that we awake to eternal life.
Amen.

generally attributed to Francis of Assisi, 1181–1226

50

"I HAVE CALLED _____
BY NAME"

Listen to the L ORD who created you. . . .
    The one who formed you says,
"Do not be afraid, for I have ransomed you.
    I have called you by name; *you are mine*.
When you go through deep waters,
    I will be with you.
When you go through rivers of difficulty,
    you will not drown.
When you walk through the fire of oppression,
    you will not be burned up;
    the flames will not consume you.
For I am the L ORD, your God,
    the Holy One of Israel, your Savior. . . .
You are precious to me.
    You are honored, and I love you."

Isaiah 43:1–4 NLT

When Ishmael was still in utero, God chose his name, "God hears," and gifted it along with the promise it implied to his mother, Hagar.

Jesus took Simon's unlikely nickname, Rock, and transformed it into both a reality and a blessing.

God renamed Abram and Jacob: Abraham and Israel.

God named Bezaleel for a specific task.

Mary, when named, knew who had spoken, even though it couldn't be possible.

In biblical times naming meant more than submitting a piece of information necessary for processing a birth certificate. The power to name meant that one had authority over the one to be named. The namer claimed responsibility for and would care for the one named. A name's meaning could reflect how the namer viewed the one being named. The prophet Isaiah writes that God has called us by name. What does that mean?

Being named is a declaration that we belong. It might be to a team, a family, or some other group. And when we belong we are not alone. Over a hundred third- and fourth-graders listened as several of their classmates volunteered to stand at the microphone and read their essays on "The Best Thing That Happened Last Summer." Nine-year-old Steve began, "The best thing that happened to me last summer was I got a new name." We teachers knew that Steve had been in seven foster homes during his young life and that his adoption had been completed during the summer. Now Steve had a new last name and a family, a place where he belonged!

Being named is an affirmation of our personhood. We each feel honored when a professor with hundreds of students or a pastor with hundreds of parishioners remembers and calls us by name. Unlike being numbered—as in a prison—being named means we are cared about, even loved.

Being named is an invitation to listen. When we hear our name in a room crowded with people who are engaged in many conversations, we listen intently, tuning out all the competing words being spoken. When someone addresses us directly by name, that person has a message or instruction intended specifically for us.

Being named is a promise to remember. During a discussion of Alzheimer's disease that took place at Church of the Servant, Ken, then in the disease's early stages, was asked, "Aren't you afraid you might even forget your own name?"

"If that happens," Ken replied, "I know God will not forget it."

People of God, we have been named by one who declares we belong to him, who walks with us even through fire and deep water. We have been told we are precious, honored, and loved. We are invited to listen, for the one who names us has work we will be empowered to do. And we have been named by one who will never forget us!

"I have called you by name; you are mine" (Isa. 43:1).

How Then Shall We Respond?

The psalmist David suggests:

Shout with joy to the LORD, all the earth!
  Worship the LORD with gladness.
  Come before him, singing with joy.
Acknowledge that the LORD is God!
  He made us, and we are his.
  We are his people, the sheep of his pasture.
Enter his gates with thanksgiving;
  go into his courts with praise.
  Give thanks to him and praise his name.
For the LORD is good.
  His unfailing love continues forever,
  and his faithfulness continues to each
  generation.

Psalm 100 NLT

*Let us love, and sing, and wonder, let us praise
  the Savior's name!*
*He has hushed the Law's loud thunder, he has
  quenched Mount Sinai's flame;*
*He has washed us with his blood, he has brought
  our souls to God.*

*Let us praise, and join the chorus of the saints
  enthroned on high;*
*Here they trusted him before us, now their praises
  fill the sky:*
*"Thou hast washed us with thy blood; thou art
  worthy, Lamb of God!" Amen.*

John Newton, "Let Us Love and Sing and Wonder," 1774

A space has been left in the title of this meditation
for your name.

Mary Foxwell Loeks grew up in Japan, the daughter of missionary parents. A graduate of Wheaton College, she taught at the elementary and preschool levels for eleven years. Mary and her husband live in Grand Rapids, Michigan, and for twenty years she served as minister of education at Church of the Servant, where she currently leads a weekly Bible study. She is the author of several books, including *Names of God*.

Begin and End Your Day in a Quiet Moment with God

Wrap Up in These Inspirational and Heartwarming Stories of Faith and Comfort

Be the First
to Hear about
Other New Books
from Revell!